Building Beloved Community in a Wounded World

D1715778

Building Beloved Community in a Wounded World

JACOB L. GOODSON
BRAD ELLIOTT STONE
PHILIP RUDOLPH KUEHNERT

CASCADE *Books* · Eugene, Oregon

Cascade Books
An Imprint of Wipf and Stock Publishers
199 W. 8th Ave., Suite 3
Eugene, OR 97401

www.wipfandstock.com

PAPERBACK ISBN: 978-1-6667-1024-3
HARDCOVER ISBN: 978-1-6667-1025-0
EBOOK ISBN: 978-1-6667-1026-7

Cataloguing-in-Publication data:

Names: Goodson, Jacob L., author. | Stone, Brad Elliott, author. | Kuehnert, Philip Rudolph, author.

Title: Building beloved community in a wounded world / Jacob L. Goodson, Brad Elliott Stone, and Philip Rudolph Kuehnert.

Description: Eugene, OR : Cascade Books, 2022 | Includes bibliographical references and index.

Identifiers: ISBN 978-1-6667-1024-3 (paperback) | ISBN 978-1-6667-1025-0 (hardcover) | ISBN 978-1-6667-1026-7 (ebook)

Subjects: LCSH: Communities—Philosophy. | Social justice—Religious aspects—Christianity. | Pragmatism.

Classification: HN31 .G66 2022 (paperback) | HN31 .G66 (ebook)

10/26/22

Again I looked and saw all the oppression that was taking place under
the sun:
I saw the tears of the oppressed—
        and they have no comforter;
power was on the side of their oppressors—
   and they have no comforter.
And I declared that the dead,
        who had already died,
are happier than the living,
        who are still alive.
But better than both
        is the one who has never been born,
who has not seen the evil
        that is done under the sun.
And I saw that all toil and all achievement spring from one person's
envy of another.
This too is meaningless, a chasing after the wind.
Fools fold their hands
        and ruin themselves.
Better one handful with tranquillity
        than two handfuls with toil and chasing after the wind.

Again I saw something meaningless under the sun:
There was a man all alone;
        he had neither son nor brother.
There was no end to his toil,
        yet his eyes were not content with his wealth.
"For whom am I toiling," he asked,
        "and why am I depriving myself of enjoyment?"
This too is meaningless—
        a miserable business!

Two are better than one,
        because they have a good return for their labor:
If either of them falls down,
        one can help the other up.
But pity anyone who falls
        and has no one to help them up.
Also, if two lie down together, they will keep warm.
        But how can one keep warm alone?
Though one may be overpowered,
        two can defend themselves.
A cord of three strands is not quickly broken. (Eccl 4:1–12)

Contents

Acknowledgments

FROM JACOB GOODSON—THIS PROJECT started midway through 2020 and it was a communal/social project from the beginning. Given the demands and restrictions of the COVID-19 pandemic, it turned out to be a real gift to have partners in thinking and writing with such limited access to other social relationships. I am grateful to both Brad and Phil for their presence (via Zoom) in my life during that time and for encouraging me to finally write on questions I have been thinking about for some time—such as the language of the cries and using the metaphor of hell for thinking through the problems of racism and white supremacy. Brad posted on Facebook that he thinks of me as a "brother from another mother," to which I concur; I fully believe that we enjoy the kind of friendship described by Aristotle in terms of the bond of *philia*.

This project was funded mostly by Phil Kuehnert; his generosity in relation to my own scholarship never ceases to amaze me, and I remain grateful for his financial support. Funding for the research also came from Larry and Linda Hahn (Winfield, KS), Alan and Annette Lindal (Wichita, KS), and Claire and Gene Partlow (Williamsburg, VA). Dr. Jackson Lashier approved funding for a trip to Los Angeles in June 2021 that proved crucial for bringing the project to completion; I am grateful for his constant encouragement and support as the Social Science Division Chair at Southwestern College.

As co-authors, we decided not to serve as editors for one another—as we thought that might blur the lines in terms of keeping our authorial voices distinct. Because of this decision, I relied on the editorial help of colleagues and friends: Deborah Allen, Stanley Hauerwas, and John Shook. As always, errors and mistakes remain my responsibility.

FROM PHILIP KUEHNERT—I OWE a debt of gratitude to John Gregoire whose influence led me out of passivity to advocacy. Three years ago, John invited me to join the planning committee of the James River Chapter of the Virginia Interfaith Center for Public Policy of Virginia. In the following three years,

John, Karen McPherson, Walter Johnson, John Whitley, Anthony Fludd, Betsy Mountcastle, Christine Payne, and Charles Swadley planned and carried out two symposia in 2019 and 2020 focused on reducing violence and building safe neighborhoods. The second symposium, held in October of 2020, was titled "Building the Beloved Community in a Wounded World" and became the inspiration behind this book. For almost three years, this group of advocates became in a very special way my beloved community.

I have a contentious relationship with writing. As I age, I seem to be writing more and enjoying it enough to continue. Along the way, my long-haul friends, Chester McCown and Timothy Thomas, have always encouraged me. In recent years, a remarkable young man has become my editor for various writing projects, including this book. I am indebted to Kelsey Knobloch for identifying and eliminating gross illiteracies as well as providing gentle questions about flow and purpose. To these three and to others who along the way have encouraged me to write, I offer my thanks.

My place in this project is at the invitation of Brad Elliott Stone and Jacob L. Goodson. I have known Jacob for ten years and have benefitted from his invitations to broaden my experience and perspective. Brad came into my life when he accepted the invitation to be one of the presenters at the fall 2020 symposium. I struggle to express the different ways that being a part of this project has challenged me to read and write beyond my comfort zone. I am still amazed at the enthusiastic way that Brad invited me, someone he barely knew, to be one of the authors. Jacob has provided the structure of the book and taken care of the many details that go with publishing a book. I am grateful to them for the opportunity. I am deeply appreciative to Professor Frederick Niedner for his career-long development of wilderness theology. His reading of the third chapter provided encouragement and clarification.

Finally, I thank God for the local congregations—the beloved communities that throughout my life have not only normalized my journey through the wilderness, but also provided me "in-place" refuge and "in-person" healing.

FROM BRAD STONE—I AM so grateful to work with Jacob Goodson and Phil Kuehnert on this book. Our conversations on the Beloved Community and mending a wounded world gave birth to this project. Jacob and I have worked with each other on many other projects and books over the years, but this was my first time working with Phil. I admire his true care for the world and for others. I found his nervousness about writing a book refreshing and invigorating (compared to a professional academic's "ho-hum, time to write"). His pastoral experience and his amazing ability to tell stories reminds those of us in the academy that the human connection is a vital part of the work we do. I also admire that Phil wanted Jacob and I to be truer to our very selves instead of wearing the costume of the publishing professor.

Since this book is about communities and the ways we try to heal the world together, I am grateful for all of the beloved communities I find myself in, and I dedicate this book to them: to my new friends in Winfield, KS, to Westwood Hills Congregational Church, to the LMU Black Community, to Holy Nativity Episcopal Church, to game groups throughout the greater Los Angeles area, to the Department of Philosophy at LMU, and to decades of beloved students and fellow scholars. Thank you for letting me participate with you.

Finally, I want to acknowledge my wife and best friend, Margaret Tuggle Stone. She has the task of creating beloved communities mostly with strangers in her position as a mental health therapist. She meets people in the midst of their tragedy and tries to instill a sense of tragicomic hope (and a big slice of reality in some cases). She truly makes the world a better place, one client at a time, and one group at a time. Thank you for giving yourself to so many forms of community.

Introduction

Jacob L. Goodson

BUILDING BELOVED COMMUNITY IN *a Wounded World* brings three distinct authorial voices together for the purpose of diagnosing the current political divisiveness in the US and to hypothesize about the significance of the phrase *beloved community* in this current moment. The opening salvo explains the urgency of the project and why a retired Lutheran pastor (Rev. Philip Kuehnert) might turn to two professional philosophers (Dr. Jacob L. Goodson and Dr. Brad Elliott Stone) out of a sense of political and social desperation.

In part 1, titled "A Wounded World," each of the authors addresses the latter part of the title for the book: *What do we mean by a wounded world?* Each author gives a different answer to this question. In chapter 1, Goodson demonstrates how philosophers in the American pragmatist tradition employ the language of cries for understanding the wounded world. In chapter 2, Stone describes the wounded world through the terminology of tragedy and the tragic. In chapter 3, Kuehnert displays theological reasoning in relation to understanding the cries heard in the wounded world.

Each author has a distinct set of conversation partners in part 1. Because of his focus on the American pragmatist tradition, Goodson explains the philosophical reasoning of Josiah Royce, William James, Hilary Putnam, Charlene Haddock Seigfried, and Cornel West. Because of his emphasis on tragedy and the tragic life, Stone engages with the thought of Sidney Hook, Miguel de Unamuno, and Cornel West. One result of Goodson's and Stone's chapters, therefore, involves making West an unavoidable thinker for understanding the significance of the wounded world. In this regard, *Building Beloved Community in a Wounded World* can be read as a sequel to *Introducing Prophetic Pragmatism: A Dialogue on Hope, the Philosophy of Race, and the Spiritual Blues.* In chapter 3, Kuenhert's primary conversation partner is the Irish philosophical theologian David Ford and his work laying out a taxonomy of cries.

In part 2, simply titled "Interventions," each of the authors addresses the former part of the title for the book: *What do we mean by beloved community?* The authors offer three different types of reflections on the phrase *beloved community.* In chapter 4, Goodson traces the phrase from its origins in the work of the American philosopher Josiah Royce through Martin Luther King Jr. to the recent use of the phrase by Joy James. In chapter 5, Stone defends an experimentalist, fallible, local, particular, and pluralistic account of beloved communities. In his chapter, Stone forces and highlights a tension between idealism and materialism when thinking about beloved community. In chapter 6, Kuehnert offers case studies for what beloved communities do and do not look like. Readers interested in the life and thought of Lutheran theologian Dietrich Bonhoeffer will find Kuehnert's argument in chapter 6 especially of interest as he reads Bonhoeffer's *Life Together* as a particular case study for understanding the dynamics of a beloved community.

Goodson and Stone dedicated two chapters to the philosophy of race in their *Introducing Prophetic Pragmatism*, and they dedicate another two chapters to the philosophy of race as the third part in this book. In chapter 7, Stone utilizes the work of two twentieth-century giants—James Baldwin and Emmanuel Levinas—to grapple with the current manifestation or situation of racism in the twenty-first century. Stone focuses on the *language* used for thinking about the problems of racism, and he recommends a shift from the language of white privilege to the French philosophical notion of *jouissance.* In a deep engagement with Stone's chapter, Goodson emphasizes a dynamic between hellishness and hopefulness in regards to race relations in the US. The result of both chapters is that, by critically examining the phrase *white privilege*, both Goodson and Stone present readers with a radically different approach—in relation to more common ways—for understanding the problems of and potential solutions for racism in the US.

Opening Salvo

Philip R. Kuehnert

"And Phil, I think you should write the opening salvo."

Salvo? A written salvo? Given the immediate context of the suggestion delivered on October 2, 2020, it made little sense. As time went on, it seemed to make less and less sense. What did not make sense was that Brad directed it at me. When asked for clarification, he responded, "It's because of you that we had to rethink what we were going to present." That philosophers, who earn their living thinking and teaching and writing about ideas that they have nurtured for decades, would be prompted to rethink their presentations by a retired pastor at a local symposium in the Tidewater area of Virginia now seems, at least, interesting.[1]

Something happened.

Ever since, I have been trying to understand the dynamics of the passion and urgency that has been unleashed: not only among the three of us but also globally. Writing now at the one year anniversary of the World Health Organization's decree that there was indeed a pandemic, those words spoken by Director-General Tedros Adhanom were indeed the opening salvo of a year of extraordinary, even unprecedented global conflict.

As you can imagine, writing this opening salvo has been quite the challenge. What follows is not an introduction to the following chapters (see Goodson's introduction for that) but, rather, an outline of the way this project has developed and the gauntlet it intends to throw down. In the first section, I will explain what I think *opening salvo* means. The second section tells the story of how this project came to be as an outcome of a symposium held in

---

1. On the nature and significance of *interesting* as a judgment within philosophy and theology, see Collier et al., "Introduction," xii–xiv.

1

the Tidewater area of Virginia. It is told with the hope that it will affirm those who have similar stories working with advocacy groups (beloved communities) as well as provide inspiration for those who need to move from idea to action. The third section attempts to explain that *something happened* in the relationship between the philosophers Stone and Goodson alongside the pastor Kuehnert. The final section again returns to the implications of salvo for all those whose ears are attentive to the cries of the wounded world: very specifically, those who knowingly, or unknowingly, wear God's ears—ears that have been attuned philosophically and theologically, ears whose hearing enter the crucible of an argument and a discourse with the intent of building and maintaining the ever-elusive Beloved Community.

SECTION 1

This is how I now understand a salvo. Salvo evokes attack—the first barrage of a continued bombardment. As a tactic in warfare, the intent is to cripple and demoralize an enemy in the initial blow—putting them in a defensive position, impairing their ability to fight back. The element of surprise is missing. Salvo carries the idea that there have been disagreements, which, unresolved, escalated until lines were drawn and armaments and defenses were established. Continuing minor skirmishes made ignoring the underlying issues impossible. It became a matter of who would initiate war, who would fire the opening salvo? Looking for examples in history, April 11, 1861, now marks the opening salvo on Fort Sumter. Almost a century of conflict between the Northern and Southern states erupted into succession and all-out war. That opening salvo erased any hope that contending issues would be resolved peaceably. All-out war was reluctantly welcomed to finally resolve the issue.

So without apology, we engage. Attack? Cripple an enemy? Engage who? And who's the *we*? As the weeks and months passed since that initial directive, the two issues that had initially prompted that symposium in Virginia metastasized. After six months of fighting the COVID-19 pandemic, the nation was unprepared for the devastation that the virus would cause in the closing months of 2020. The racial unrest of George Floyd's whispered cry, "I can't breathe," prompted a worldwide response from many oppressed peoples. His cry also prompted widespread demonstrations in the US that often became violent and destructive. Election day provided a brief yet uneasy respite that was quickly dissipated as the results of the election were rejected. All this culminated in the events that have placed the date of January 6 with the dates December 7 and September 11.

Attack? Well, yes! In the same way that the Old Testament prophets unleashed what can be called an unrelenting bombardment on the peoples of Judah and Israel, the opening salvo again and again was, "The Word of the Lord came . . ." The narrow focus of the attack was the idolatry that resulted in widespread injustice and oppression of the poor. I hope that we, the co-authors of this book, echo the passion and the urgency of the Old Testament prophets as they communicated judgment and mercy. In some sense, I hope that *the Word of the Lord*—which continually confronts us in our worshiping lives—provides the fire of the Holy Spirit to maintain our passion and sustain the urgency.

The enemy? If there is a common denominator in the base line of what ails between those who are philosophers and those who carry a pastoral identity, it is the humility to know and acknowledge that we are as much the enemy as those who we identify as the enemy.[2] However, we refuse to let this truth immobilize or mute us. We do not agree on the identity of the primary enemy. We admit our complicity with the hope that what we write will be read as a form of confession. For those who have lost their voice because of the disorienting nature of the present wilderness, we hope that we—at least in part—speak for them. For those who want to join in building the beloved community in a wounded world, we hope to identify those critical issues—as did the Old Testament prophets—that lead to repentance and, more importantly, to restoration and reconciliation.

Engage who? You the reader and all the wounded in this wounded world. This will be a difficult book for most readers. It will be the exceptional reader that will be comfortable with the dense philosophical writings—from different perspectives—of Professors Stone and Goodson, as well as the rather parochial world of a Christian/Lutheran beloved community of Kuehnert. For many, the work needed to follow the arguments may not be worth the time. I can relate to the despair of trying to follow finely tuned arguments that use words and terminology that are not part of my personal lexicon. For others, the pain of thinking deeply about the cries of the wounded—especially the cries that echo personal cries—will be too hurtful. For others still, the theology that I claim to be inseparable from the concept of the Beloved Community, but necessary for building it and effectively responding to the cacophony of cries rising up from our wounded world, may be offensive. Given the diversity of perspectives represented, we hope there may be several ways this book engages you.

To be clear, this book provides two tracks: the first in the philosophical tension between idealism and materialism, and the second theologically

---

2. Goodson, "The Psalms of Vengeance."

between the ideal of the holy Christian church and actual worshiping communities of saints and sinners. The three of us challenge you to think deeply, to expand your understanding and your internalized lexicon, and to renew your commitment to do your part in building the beloved community in our wounded world. Given the depressing accumulation of debris from centuries of failures to establish and maintain beloved communities (or, simply, communities), we—Goodson, Stone, Kuehnert—have general consensus that engaging in rigorous arguments about beloved community from two different philosophical perspectives, as well as my own pastoral approach, will provide a fresh look at the ingredients necessary for building beloved community in a wounded world. Our trust is that the reader will have the intellectual resources and the communal courage to create a provisional recipe of what that beloved community might look like at *this time* and in *this place*.

SECTION 2

The story of how the suggestion "And Phil, I think that you . . ." of October 2 began goes back more than two years. In the fall of 2018, I was invited to be part of the planning committee of the James River Chapter of the Virginia Interfaith Center for Public Policy (VICPP). The only person I knew at that first meeting was John G., who invited me to join. Although VICPP has been around for decades, I was new to its purpose and its organization. Those I met were a diverse group of bright veterans of the fight for social justice in the Tidewater area of Virginia. The group seemed to be needing something to plan. A longtime acquaintance, an activist with the Sierra Club in the state of Washington, had shared with me a model of engaging and promoting disparate civic and religious organizations through an annual meeting. That annual meeting—involving multiple civic, religious, and nonprofit organizations—was sponsored by an organization similar to VICPP. That model was the spark that our group needed. We decided to plan a symposium for the fall of 2019. Creative juices flowed. Looking back, it certainly was ambitious, but the extensive networks that our group brought together—along with the contacts that my colleagues had developed over the years—provided the resources needed to continue planning. The group struggled to get beyond a "this is what is wrong, let's fix it" mentality to explore the components of vibrant and nurturing communities. The decision was made to sponsor a symposium, named "Healthy Communities Reduce and Prevent Violence." One member of the planning group offered his church, Zion Prospect Baptist Church in Yorktown, as the meeting place for the event. The symposium featured three keynote speakers, an interfaith panel on violence, and six breakout sessions. Late into the planning process, the decision was made to break the symposium into two parts: one meeting in September and one in October.

The symposium accomplished its objectives. The planning group was encouraged by the support it received: over twenty religious and civic organizations signed on as sponsors, and the number of participants met expectations. In addition, the overwhelmingly positive comments in evaluations provided ideas for future planning.

In February of 2020, the planning group gathered once again. There was no debate as to whether or not to sponsor another symposium. Plans were in the very initial stages when, in the middle of March, Virginia was shut down because of the pandemic. Our meetings, now on Zoom, soon became weekly. Necessity bred creativity. Of course, whatever we planned would need to be virtual—probably on the Zoom platform. None of the decisions were easy. What would be the primary focus? How would publicity be different from the previous year? What limitations and what additional options were available with a virtual symposium? Would the symposium be two hours, three, four, or more? Who would be the keynote speakers? Most decisions were arrived at only after considering many options. Strong leadership emerged in the group, depending on the need. By this time, most in the group had known each other and had worked together for more than a year. Yet, we knew very little about our lives outside the group, much less our personal histories.

A turning point in the group was when I suggested that we share our personal stories. Not knowing what to expect, I was surprised as one after another shared their personal histories. Career trajectories. Successes and failures. Diverse family of origin stories. Religious pilgrimages. From that point on, the planning group began taking on another dimension. In my mind, subconsciously, I began claiming the group as one of my beloved communities.

By early summer, important decisions had been made. The focus would be the twin crises of racial unrest and the pandemic. Obviously, the world was wounded. The title would be, "Building the Beloved Community in a Wounded World." Two keynote speakers were identified and signed on. The symposium would start mid-morning and conclude early afternoon. One of the planning group members who had extensive experience with 4-H suggested that we organize the day with 5-Hs: heroes, honor, health, healing, and hope. Each H was taken by a member of the group with the understanding that the topic would be developed independently of the others, but ought to remain within the forty-minute time frame allotted to each.

SECTION 3

I took the final topic: hope. I soon became quite anxious about how to develop it for the symposium. Others seemed to have instantaneous ideas and accessible resources for their part of the symposium, but I struggled. It had been some time since Jacob Goodson and I had been in contact. I remembered that, in some of his writings, hope had been the focus. I called him and asked him if he would be willing to be part of the symposium. Almost immediately, he accepted—with the provision that he could invite his friend and fellow philosopher and co-author, Brad Elliott Stone, to join him. Their assignment was to prepare and present a ten- to fifteen-minute presentation on hope and the beloved community.

Shortly after that, the three of us decided to meet weekly on Fridays to discuss options. It was now the end of August. The symposium, scheduled for October 7, was just weeks away. It seemed that Stone and Goodson were primed for the assignment. They had recently (2019) published a co-authored book: *Introducing Prophetic Pragmatism: A Dialogue on Hope, the Philosophy of Race, and the Spiritual Blues.* They accepted the assignment and soon exhibited enthusiasm for the topic. As I listened in—really, *overheard*—their conversation, it was obvious that both of them were conversant in the concept of beloved community not only in Martin Luther King's preaching and writing, but even more in the origins of the concept of beloved community as developed by a primary influence of Martin Luther King Jr.'s thinking: the turn-of-the-century American philosopher Josiah Royce. I was surprised by the enthusiasm that they exhibited for the topic.

By the third Friday, I realized that both Brad and Jacob were well into their assignments. The week before, they had provided detailed outlines of their presentations and, on this Friday, they shared written manuscripts of their presentations. I was impressed. At that point, two things happened. They began talking about a book "that needed to written—and soon!" Second, I noticed that their finely crafted academic writing lacked any reference to their experiences in beloved communities. I was afraid that, given the expected participants for the symposium, their presentations would not be well received. I have known Jacob, his wife, his two children, and his mother for over nine years—first as a fellow member of a worshiping community in Williamsburg, Virginia; then as a partner in teaching several multi-class Sunday morning bible classes; and, finally, as a participant in the Society of Scriptural Reasoning.[3] An ongoing and contentious part of

---

3. Scriptural Reasoning (SR) is a tool for inter-faith dialogue whereby people of different faiths come together to read and reflect on their Scriptures. Since 2008, Jacob L. Goodson has served as the general editor for the *Journal of Scriptural Reasoning*. See his work at https://jsr.shanti.virginia.edu.

our relationship had been my begging for his voice to be heard in what he wrote. He defended his style, sometimes stridently, stating that it was not the way he was trained to write. But I knew enough of his history to know that *community* played an important part in his family's life. So hesitantly, I asked if he could include more of his story.

About Brad I knew much less, but what I knew was intriguing. He was raised in an interracial farming community in Kentucky where neighbors were, well, neighbors. In addition, he presented himself in an almost folksy way. His personal history included positive elements of community, and I wanted to know more. Also, he hinted that he was a part of two worshiping communities. I was very curious. The result was that each revised their presentations, including their personal stories as related to communities. I was quite excited.

On October 2, my co-authors, the philosophers Brad Elliott Stone and Jacob L. Goodson, and I had been meeting weekly on six consecutive Fridays. Our final meeting on this Friday was, like the others, on Zoom—with Stone in Los Angeles, Goodson in Kansas, and me in Virginia. It was more of a celebration and final preparation for the symposium than a meeting. Tongue in cheek, I asked when "the book" would be published. To my surprise, Stone quickly named four or five chapters in the book. It was obvious that there had been much thinking about the topic. Adding to my surprise, it seemed they had assumed that I would be part of this co-authored book. I was hesitant for several reasons. While I love to write, I know my limitations. To be included in a volume with published academic philosophers seemed to me to reflect unfair expectations. They were insistent. They felt that my perspective as a pastor/pastoral psychotherapist was needed. Then, "And Phil, I think you should write the opening salvo."

SECTION 4

Once again: given the depressing accumulation of debris from centuries of failures to establish and maintain beloved communities, we—Goodson, Stone, Kuehnert—have general consensus that engaging in rigorous arguments about the concept of beloved community from two different philosophical perspectives and a pastoral approach will provide a fresh look at the ingredients necessary for beloved community to happen. Our trust is that the reader will have the intellectual resources and the communal courage to create a provisional recipe of what that beloved community might look like for them at *this time* and in *this place*.

Beloved communities are fragile. Beloved communities can be seemingly indestructible, but of course they are not. Some beloved communities become toxic. Toxic communities can wound members, some to the extent that the wounded will never again trust themselves to the group process or to any type of community. Beloved communities have often been miraculous in providing healing. And so, beloved communities totter between the toxic and the therapeutic.

Beloved communities are people gathering for a specific reason. While this book is primarily an in-depth exploration of the more or less formal idea and construct of the Beloved Community from contemporary philosophical and theological perspectives, there is no attempt to provide a comprehensive survey of the ways beloved communities have evolved through the centuries. Beloved communities through the ages have been the incubators of thought and places of refuge. Exploration of that evolution will prove to be fascinating and instructive. Such a survey would trace the histories of communities as recorded in the Abrahamic Scriptures as well as generations of diverse groups that have used those Scriptures as inspiration. From Jewish history, we know of the competing rabbinic schools of Hillel and Shammai and how those influences continue to pollinate the vibrancy of contemporary Judaism. In a similar vein, the Islamic tradition has evolved into many different expressions. In the Christian tradition, the New Testament hints at the rival communities of first-century Judaism that we know as the Essenes, Sadducees, Pharisees, and Zealots. The Gospels document Jesus' seeming failed attempts to form a beloved community of his disciples. With Pentecost galvanizing that first group, the Acts of the Apostles as told by Luke does not hide the messiness of the start-up Christian church. The Epistles record the attempts by their authors to coach those fledgling beloved communities not only to survive, but to truly be beloved communities. Into the common era, both the Christian and the Jewish traditions demonstrate never-ending experiments to establish the Beloved Community on earth.

President Biden addressing the nation on March 11, 2021, the first anniversary of the COVID-19 shutdown began by acknowledging how important it is for people to be together. In the biblical record, the first thing that God names "not good" is loneliness. Groups are ubiquitous: from self-help groups to attempts at communal living to the more or less formally constituted groups, ranging from fan clubs for celebrities and sports teams to service clubs. In my lifetime, I have seen small groups come and go—with some proving amazingly successful. The best known is Alcoholic Anonymous (AA), which has spawned numerous twelve-step groups addressing various forms of addiction. As a pastoral counselor in training, I was part of several groups ranging from peer supervision to group supervision to didactic groups to inter-personal relations (IPR) groups. As a pastoral counselor for some twenty-five years, I found it necessary to continue to be part of peer consultation groups in which I presented cases for consultation as well as providing consultation for other counselors. In my work as a pastoral psychotherapist, I was attracted to the promise of Sensitivity and Training Groups (Esalen Institute, etc.). Therapy groups and support groups continue to provide beloved communities in formal and informal, inpatient and outpatient treatment settings. As a pastor, I initiated small-group ministry in my congregations in Atlanta and Fairbanks.

As we hope our writing illustrates, what we are describing and what we think is the genius behind the idea that Josiah Royce first described and that Martin Luther King Jr. claimed as part of his dream is elusive but at least in part attainable. With foreshadowing in the covenantal people of the Old Testament, the disciples who became apostles, the disparate religious communities through the centuries, and the explosion of religious groups in the nineteenth and twentieth centuries, attempting to build the elusive and mystical Beloved Community is worth the effort. Not to do so is to ignore the primary call of God to God's creation to be God's ears, God's eyes, and God's hands on earth.

However you want to interpret it—whether as a wake-up call, or the admission that you have given up on finding a trustworthy community, or that you live with broken integrity, or simply taking a closer look at the communities you are a part of—whether family, congregation, neighborhood, workplace, volunteer group, or service organization, it is critically important on every level, from the intensely personal, to the local, regional, national, and global that the Beloved Community be the place, primarily local, where we are not only nurtured and cared for, but also where we with others join to do that which we cannot do by ourselves: to be a reconciling and redemptive presence in the world.

PART 1

A Wounded World

1

Understanding the Wounded World through the Language of Cries

Jacob L. Goodson

In all the songs of the forest birds; in all the cries of the wounded and dying, struggling in the captor's power; in the boundless sea, where the myriads of water-creatures strive and die; amid all the countless hordes of savage men; in the hearts of all the good and loving; in the dull, throbbing hearts of all prisoners and captives; in all sickness and sorrow; in all exultation of hope; in all our devotion; in all our knowledge—everywhere from the lowest to the noblest creatures and experiences on our earth, the same conscious, burning, willful life is found, endlessly manifold as the forms of the living creatures, unquenchable as the fires of the sun, real as these impulses that even now throb in thy own little selfish heart.[1]

---

1. Royce, *The Religious Aspects of Philosophy*, 161–62.

INTRODUCTION

In one of his early works, *The Religious Aspect of Philosophy: A Critique of the Bases of Conduct and of Faith*, Josiah Royce (1855–1916) outlines the content of and reasons for a religious philosophy. Royce considers his thinking as a religious philosophy because he defends an Absolute Knower or Absolute Mind (Royce's actual term is "Infinite Mind"[2])—who shares the traditional attributes of the Christian God. This becomes part and parcel of his defense and elaboration of absolute idealism—briefly discussed later in this chapter.

In the present chapter, I will explore in detail what Royce means by the phrase "cries of the wounded"—found in his seminal text, *The Religious Aspect of Philosophy*.[3] Second, I explain Royce's absolute idealism. Third, I take up how Royce's colleague at Harvard University—William James (1842–1910)—utilizes the same phrase in two of his essays: "The Moral Philosopher and the Moral Life," and "On a Certain Blindness in Human Beings." Fourth, I remain with James's work and connect the phrase "cries of the wounded" with the religious categories of the divided self and sick soul found in James's *The Varieties of Religious Experience*.[4] I conclude by looking to three contemporary pragmatists and their usage of the phrase: Hilary Putnam (1926–2016), Charlene Haddock Seigfried (1943–), and Cornel West (1953–).

In essence, in this chapter I attempt to think through the notion of the wounded world through pragmatist uses of the language of cries. I demonstrate that American pragmatists turn toward the language of cries in order to reflect upon the wounded world. The thesis of the chapter is twofold. From Royce's philosophy, we learn that listening to the cries of the wounded requires distinguishing between legitimate and illegitimate cries.[5] From James's philosophy, we learn that listening to the cries of the wounded ought to be understood on the terms of vocation; I argue that once we commit to the vocation of listening to the cries of the wounded, it leads to becoming either a divided self or a sick soul.[6]

2. Royce, *The Religious Aspects of Philosophy*, 446.

3. Royce, *The Religious Aspects of Philosophy*, 161.

4. See James, *The Varieties of Religious Experience*, lectures XI and XII.

5. I am in debt to John Shook for clarifying this as my first thesis for this chapter; Shook recommends calling illegitimate cries, on Royce's standards, whining—not crying!

6. This second thesis statement involves my disagreement with Sami Pihlström's argument in "The Cries of the Wounded in *Pragmatism*," that being a sick soul leads to listening to the cries of the wounded; I argue that listening to the cries of the wounded leads to becoming either a divided self or a sick soul.

JOSIAH ROYCE'S *THE RELIGIOUS ASPECT OF PHILOSOPHY*

Royce published *The Religious Aspect of Philosophy* in 1885, while he was an instructor at Harvard University. According to his intellectual biographer, Bruce Kuklick, Royce wrote *The Religious Aspect of Philosophy* in order to demonstrate how American pragmatism and German idealism apply to religious questions.[7] In Kuklick's words: "He [Royce] devotes a large portion of *The Religious Aspect of Philosophy* to a survey of religious problems because they first drove him to philosophy."[8] This does not mean, however, that the book represents Royce's personal struggles: "he urges that his philosophy depends in no way on his personal concerns."[9] In relation to these religious questions and problems, Kuklick claims two accomplishments found in Royce's *The Religious Aspect of Philosophy*. First, the "argument from the possibility of error . . . established the young Harvard instructor as one of the leading proponents of philosophical idealism."[10] Second, Royce applies William James's and C. S. Peirce's pragmatism more concretely to religious problems and questions than either of them (James or Peirce) had achieved by 1885: "Royce was a pragmatist . . . , [and] . . . the doctrine advanced there [in *The Religious Aspect of Philosophy*] is pragmatic in its emphasis on the intentionality of judgment, in the idea that judgment chooses, picks out, or means its object."[11] For purposes of this chapter, I agree with Kuklick's evaluation of Royce's *The Religious Aspect of Philosophy*. In the first subsection, I focus on the pragmatist aspect of Royce's use of the phrase "cries of the wounded"; in the second subsection, I briefly touch on the idealist aspect of Royce's use of the phrase.

Royce on "the Cries of the Wounded"

There is one passage in Royce's *The Religious Aspect of Philosophy* often overlooked, and I draw attention to it as a point of reflection for this chapter.[12]

7. Through personal correspondence, Stanley Hauerwas recommended that I clarify this even more and say that Royce sees himself as building from G. W. F. Hegel's idealism more so than German Idealism in general (Hauerwas, personal correspondence with the author, June 9, 2021).

8. Kuklick, *Josiah Royce*, 25.

9. Kuklick, *Josiah Royce*, 25.

10. Kuklick, *Josiah Royce*, 37.

11. Kuklick, *Josiah Royce*, 40.

12. My basic strategy for writing on Royce in this chapter involves taking what three different Royce scholars (i.e., Kuklick, Parker, Trotter) say about his philosophical

While some of it is quoted as the epigraph for the beginning of this chapter, I quote the whole passage here:

> Hatred is illusion. Cowardly sympathy, that hides its head for fear of realizing the neighbor's pain, is illusion. But unselfishness is the realization of life. Unselfishness leads thee out of the mists of blind self-adoration . . . In all the songs of the forest birds; in all the cries of the wounded and dying, struggling in the captor's power; in the boundless sea, where the myriads of water-creatures strive and die; amid all the countless hordes of savage men; in the hearts of all the good and loving; in the dull, throbbing hearts of all prisoners and captives; in all sickness and sorrow; in all exultation of hope; in all our devotion; in all our knowledge—everywhere from the lowest to the noblest creatures and experiences on our earth, the same conscious, burning, willful life is found, endlessly manifold as the forms of the living creatures, unquenchable as the fires of the sun, real as these impulses that even now throb in thy own little selfish heart. Lift up thy eyes, behold that life, and then turn away and forget it as thou canst; but if thou has known that, thou hast begun to know thy duty.[13]

Philosophical writing does not get much more poetic than Royce achieves in this passage. In typical analytic fashion, however, I break from the poetry of the prose and turn it into a logical argument with several premises and a conclusion. Admittedly, the conclusion that I draw abstracts and highlights "cries of the wounded" based upon my own interests and purposes.

First, from hatred to unselfishness: Royce treats unselfishness as what opposes hatred. The alternative to hate becomes unselfishness and—eventually—following one's duty.[14] The problem with hatred is epistemological: hatred is always based upon an illusion about how the world is—the reality

---

reasoning and applying their explanations and interpretations to his use of the phrase "cries of the wounded." In what I read, I could not find any substantive explanations and interpretations of Royce's use of this phrase. Hence, why I claim this passage is overlooked.

13. Royce, *The Religious Aspects of Philosophy*, 161–62.

14. Griffin Trotter offers some historical background to Royce's move here: "It is no surprise that Royce, a self-professed California contrarian and admirer of Immanuel Kant, began his discussion of the moral life by insisting that morality is a matter of duty and that doing one's duty means following one's path" (Trotter, *On Royce*, 26). For Royce, "following one's path" can be judged as ethical or moral when and only when it remains void of selfishness, as well. Hence Trotter's connection between Royce's Californian upbringing alongside his admiration of Kant's notion of duty: yes, follow your own path (the Californian ideal), but do so without it involving selfishness (the Kantian ideal).

of the world. Another illusion, perhaps more obvious as an illusion, involves hiding one's "head for fear of realizing the neighbor's pain"—what I label as indifference to the cries of the wounded.[15] Royce treats both hatred and indifference as illusions: epistemological problems that fail to acknowledge the reality or realities of the world.

Royce's treatment of both hatred and indifference as illusions leads to one of the pragmatist aspects of Royce's argument. What do I mean by the pragmatist aspect of Royce's argument? Again, in Kuklick's words, "the doctrine advanced there [in *The Religious Aspect of Philosophy*] is pragmatic in its emphasis on the intentionality of judgment, in the idea that judgment chooses, picks out, or means its object."[16] Both hatred and indifference prevent proper judgment. In relation to the cries of the wounded, this results in two different insights: (a) those who are full of hatred or remain indifferent cannot hear the cries of the wounded, and (b) those who are full of hatred or remain indifferent cannot, themselves, cry out as wounded because what they think of as their own wounds ought to be judged as the product or result of their own illusions about reality. Royce draws a line in the sand here: the wounds of those full of hatred are not really wounds but are only thought to be wounds based upon the illusions such people carry around with them about reality.

Second, what is unselfishness? Epistemologically, unselfishness tunes one into the realities of the world. Royce's words for this are: "unselfishness is the realization of life."[17] As such, unselfishness "leads [one] out of the mists of blind self-adoration."[18] Unselfishness helps one see the world properly, and it orients one to a moral understanding of those within the world.

Griffin Trotter, who published one of the clearest and simplest introductions to Royce's philosophy, sees Royce's argument about unselfishness in terms of a specific kind of moral development. Trotter's version of Roycean moral development looks like this:

> At the first level, our moral horizons are narrow and our only pressing concern is personal gratification. At this stage the life plan revolves around ordering various selfish desires so as to effect their maximal overall fulfillment. At the second level, we come to cherish the lives of some of our closest fellow creatures—often members of our family or some cultural group. At this stage, our life plan is no longer so self-centered, but it is still

15. See Royce, *The Religious Aspects of Philosophy*, 161.

16. Kuklick, *Josiah Royce*, 40.

17. Royce, *The Religious Aspects of Philosophy*, 161.

18. Royce, *The Religious Aspects of Philosophy*, 161.

selfish insofar as the ideals of our favored group are the only ones that matter to us. Other groups are not a factor. Finally, at the third level, we achieve a capacity for genuine loyalty. Though we are still faithful to our natural communities, we now experience the legitimacy of others' communities and strive to bring the destiny of our own group into harmony with that of others.[19]

Trotter's version of Roycean moral development leads to a connection between building beloved community and listening to the cries of the wounded: building beloved community is conditioned on learning to listen to the cries of the wounded, and listening to the cries of the wounded is conditioned on individual transition and personal transformation from selfishness to unselfishness. This individual transition and personal transformation includes coming to see other communities as equally legitimate as one's own community. Ultimately, the individual transition and personal transformation from selfishness to unselfishness results in striving "to bring the destiny of our own group into harmony with that of others."[20] Why should we learn to listen to the cries of the wounded? Because it becomes a necessary condition for building beloved community.

Third, coming to see the world rightly involves seeing the world with many of its difficult, surprising, and wonderful features—which turns out to be what Royce's very lengthy, yet poetic, sentence is all about. I give a sample of some of the difficult, surprising, and wonderful features: songs of the forest birds, the striving and struggles of fish and other animals living in water; sickness, sorrow, and suffering of different types of human beings (like prisoners); and devotion, hope, and knowledge among all types of human beings—no matter their plight in life.

Listening to the cries of the wounded involves listening to the sickness, sorrow, and suffering of particular human beings. Listening to the cries of the wounded also involves a certain type of orientation within the world— an orientation of appreciating difficulty, being surprised by particular features of the world, and coming to a place of wonder within the world. Yes, philosophy begins in wonder (Plato); listening to the cries of the wounded also requires wonder (Royce).

Fourth, unselfishness empowers one to "know thy duty."[21] For Royce, coming to know one's duty means seeing the world rightly. If you see the world through your own hatred and indifference, then you will never be able to see the world rightly. If you see the world through unselfishness, then

---

19. Trotter, *On Royce*, 41.

20. Trotter, *On Royce*, 41.

21. Royce, *The Religious Aspects of Philosophy*, 161.

you will be able to see the world rightly. Seeing the world rightly allows one to know their duty.

What is our primary duty? In answering this question, I abstract and highlight one part of Royce's passage based upon my own interests and purposes. To come to know one's duty involves listening for the "cries of the wounded and dying."[22] Why does he couch this phrase between two points about animals—the birds in the air and the fish in the sea? Because *one knows that one knows their duty* when one can hear the cries of the wounded as clearly and often as one hears the birds of the air and sees the fish in the sea. For Royce, the ethical life requires *listening* for the cries of the wounded and being able to *see* those who are actually wounded. For Royce, to see the world rightly is not to see a wounded world in the abstract, but to see actual people who are wounded in the concrete. To talk about the wounded world, therefore, requires the following insight: *the wounded world should be understood as actual wounded people, and we should resist the move to abstraction about who is wounded.*[23]

Although he does not repeat the phrase "cries of the wounded" in *The Religious Aspect of Philosophy*, he does elaborate more on woundedness. He claims that the wounds of one individual signal the failure of "universal reason" because woundedness results from an "irrational wrong."[24] Those who are wounded are wounded because of some "irrational wrong" done to them.[25] When we listen for the cries of the wounded, therefore, we are listening for those who have been wronged in irrational ways. Such a claim leads us to Royce's absolute idealism.

Royce's Absolute Idealism

In Royce's absolute idealism, error gets connected with irrationality and truth with divine rationality. In the entry on Royce's philosophy in the *Stanford Encyclopedia of Philosophy*, Kelly Parker explains the plain sense of Royce's position, known as absolute idealism:

22. Royce, *The Religious Aspects of Philosophy*, 161.

23. Griffin Trotter claims that Royce remained very aware of the accusation about abstraction in his thinking: "He [Royce] begins to articulate his response to his critics (such as Peirce and James) who suggested that his theory was mere abstraction, devoid of major practical implications. Royce argues that his theory of the Absolute provides a foundation for the articulation of personal aims" (Trotter, *On Royce*, 19).

24. See Royce, *The Religious Aspects of Philosophy*, 263.

25. See Royce, *The Religious Aspects of Philosophy*, 263.

Royce announced the beginning of his professional career with a novel defense of absolute idealism, "the argument from error." . . . In *The Religious Aspect of Philosophy*, Royce took the experience of error—a particularly compelling aspect of the phenomenon of knowing—as the starting point for his own transcendental argument. According to the correspondence theory of knowledge, an idea (or judgment) is true if it correctly represents its object; error obtains when an idea does not correctly represent its object. It is indisputable that finite minds do sometimes entertain erroneous ideas. Royce pointed out that in such a case, the mind must contain an (erroneous) idea and its (false) object, while simultaneously intending, or "pointing toward," the idea's true object. If the mind is able to intend the true object then that object is somehow available to the mind. How can it be that the true object is in this way available to the mind, but not known? Consider what happens in an ordinary example of error: if I think that my keys are on the table, but later discover that they are in my pocket, I do not conclude that my keys never existed as the object of my thought. Rather, I focus on an idea that I had all along—that my keys do definitely exist somewhere. The keys, their location, and all other facts about them are the true object of an idea. At the moment when I discover that my keys are not on the table, it becomes apparent that this true object was only imperfectly available to me. The fact that such error does occur indicated to Royce that the true object of any idea must exist, in a fully determinate or absolute state, in some actual mind with which my own mind is or may be connected. From the possibility of error, Royce concluded that there is an Absolute Knower, a mind for which all thoughts do correspond correctly and adequately to their true objects.[26]

What is the connection between Royce's use of the phrase "cries of the wounded" and his defense of absolute idealism? Those who are wounded are wounded because of the error or errors of others—which is why he calls woundedness a result of an "irrational wrong."[27] For Royce, no judgment can be made about wounds or woundedness if there is not an absolute standard—an ideal—that allows us to make such a judgment. Otherwise, claiming woundedness remains an arbitrary opinion.[28] While I do not tend to agree with Royce's absolute idealism *in toto*, I agree with *this aspect* of

26. Parker, "Josiah Royce."

27. See Royce, *The Religious Aspects of Philosophy*, 263.

28. For Royce's critique of arbitrary opinions, see *The Religious Aspects of Philosophy*, 390–96.

Royce's idealism: learning to listen to the cries of the wounded involves constantly making judgments about legitimate versus illegitimate wounds, and figuring out this distinction requires avoiding arbitrary opinion both in regards to who cries and in regards to who listens to the cries. This absolute standard is held or possessed by an Absolute Knower—what Royce calls an "Infinite Mind."[29] (I do not agree with this aspect of Royce's absolute idealism.) In his absolute idealism, therefore, Royce connects error-with-woundedness and truth-with-the-divine.

What does it mean to connect error-with-woundedness? According to Bruce Kuklick, "Royce defines . . . error as an 'incomplete thought': a higher thought which includes the error and its intended object knows the error to have failed in the purpose that it more or less clearly had."[30] These types of error result in brokenness and woundedness. In other words, the wounds experienced by actual people result from "irrational wrongs" that impact actual persons and real relationships.[31] Royce's connection of error-with-woundedness means that listening to the cries of the wounded requires serious and thoughtful discernment: not all cries are legitimate cries, but legitimate cries ought to be heard because they are the result of irrationality. In the end, Royce thinks irrationality will be cleaned up.

Lastly, concerning Royce's absolute idealism, what does it mean to connect truth-with-the-divine? According to scholars of Royce's philosophy, answering this question wholly depends upon which "country" determines Royce's thinking most concretely: Germany or the US? Royce's understanding of God goes between G.W.F. Hegel's (German) view of God and C. S. Peirce's (American) view of God. Trotter puts it in the clearest terms: "Many of Royce's contemporaries thought of his philosophy as Hegel's last gasp . . . because both were absolute idealists," but Royce does not agree with Hegel's view of God as "a man of war."[32] Trotter clarifies Royce's sentiment about Hegel's view of God: "Though Royce agrees [with Hegel] that human fulfillment can be achieved only through strenuous effort, suffering and travail, he does not subscribe wholeheartedly to the metaphor of battle [found in Hegel's view of God]."[33] Furthermore, according to Trotter, "Royce's comments on Hegel tend to portray the German idealist as an intellectual bully, more concerned with establishing his own position in the

---

29. Royce, *The Religious Aspects of Philosophy*, 446.

30. Kuklick, *Josiah Royce*, 36.

31. See Royce, *The Religious Aspects of Philosophy*, 263.

32. Trotter, *On Royce*, 22; quoting Royce, *The Spirit of Modern Philosophy*, 214.

33. Trotter, *On Royce*, 22–23.

academic hierarchy than with expressing the humility and sensitivity of sublime religion."[34] Trotter concludes that Royce's view of God remains closer to the American philosopher C. S. Peirce's.[35] What defines and determines Peirce's view of God? Peirce's view of God is defined and determined by his position known as *agapeism*: God has a loving relationship with the world in such a way that God makes *agape* love a natural and necessary feature of the world in terms of how creatures relate to one another.[36] If Royce is more Peircean than Hegelian in his view of God, then listening to the cries of the wounded becomes one of the ways that human beings manifest the natural and necessary feature of *agape* love within the world.[37] Listening to the cries of the wounded connects truth claims about the world with the love God has for the world.[38] In the end, because of God's love for the world, falsity and irrationality will be cleaned up and fully resolved.

WILLIAM JAMES'S USE OF "CRIES OF THE WOUNDED"

In "The Moral Philosopher and the Moral Life," William James uses Royce's phrase, but with neither quotation nor citation. James uses the phrase specifically in relation to the limitations and vocation of philosophy. He writes,

> The philosopher . . . *qua* philosopher . . . is no better able to determine the best universe in the concrete emergency than other [people]. He sees, indeed, somewhat better than most . . . what the question always is—not a question of this good or that good simply taken, but of the two total universes with which these goods are respectively belong. He knows that he must vote always for the richer universe, for the good which seems most organizable, most fit to enter complex combinations, most apt to be a member of a more inclusive whole. But which particular universe this is he cannot know for certain in advance; he only

---

34. Trotter, *On Royce*, 23.

35. See Trotter, *On Royce*, 23.

36. See Peirce, "Evolutionary Love," 352–72.

37. Interestingly, Peirce read Royce's *The Religious Aspect of Philosophy* as an Hegelian argument. According to Trotter, "Royce's initial version of the Absolute shares many similarities with Hegel's. In fact, Charles Peirce called Royce's first book on absolute idealism, *The Religious Aspect of Philosophy*, 'an excellent introduction to Hegel'" (Trotter, *On Royce*, 13).

38. Although not relevant to the current project, I wish to distance myself from Royce's critique of Hegel and his view of God as a "man of war" (see Royce, *The Spirit of Modern Philosophy*, 214). Hegel's view of God is much more complex than Royce presents.

knows that if he makes a bad mistake, the cries of the wounded
will soon inform him of the fact.[39]

James unnecessarily genders the philosopher in this passage, only using
the masculine pronoun to describe who the philosopher is. James's use of
the phrase in this passage signals that the cries of the wounded holds philosophers into account. Although philosophers do see people "better than
most" do, when philosophers make mistakes—when philosophers fail to see
people rightly—then "the cries of the wounded will soon inform [the phi-
losopher] of [that] fact."[40] I infer from this that one way to describe the vocation of philosophy involves attending to the cries of the wounded, because
ignoring or neglecting such cries signals a failure of the philosophical task.

In another essay written around the same time, "On a Certain Blindness in Human Beings," James again adopts and utilizes Royce's phrase:
"cries of the wounded." This time, however, James actually quotes and cred-
its Royce with the phrase. James links listening to the cries of the wounded
with what he calls a needed change within all individual human beings:

> Yet we are but finite, and each one of us has some single spe-
> cialized vocation of his own. And it seems as if energy in the
> service of its particular duties might be got only by hardening
> the heart . . . , [but eventually] the hard externality give[s] way,
> and a gleam of insight into the ejective world . . . , the vast world
> of inner life beyond us, so different from that of outer seeming,
> illuminate[s] our mind. Then the whole scheme of our custom-
> ary values gets confounded, then our self is riven and its narrow
> interests fly to pieces, then a new center and a new perspective
> must be found.[41]

For James, the change concerns the way we think of our duties or obligations. On my interpretation of this essay, the cries of the wounded represent
what James calls "the hard externality" in the above quotation.[42] Thereby
the cries of the wounded shift our understanding of duty from that of our
"specialized vocation" to knowing that our duty ought to be directed toward
those who are wounded.[43] James's claim is that, for each of us, our vocations
need such a challenge.

---

39. W. James, "The Moral Philosopher and the Moral Life," 210.
40. W. James, "The Moral Philosopher and the Moral Life," 210.
41. W. James, "On a Certain Blindness in Human Beings," 119.
42. W. James, "On a Certain Blindness in Human Beings," 119.
43. See W. James, "On a Certain Blindness in Human Beings," 119.

In James's philosophy, individuals have the ability to will themselves to religious belief, to will themselves to continue to live, and even to will themselves to believe in free will! In "On a Certain Blindness in Human Beings," however, James seems to slam the breaks on his faith in the human will—on his philosophical voluntarism. We cannot and do not will ourselves out of complacency, but rather, need "hard external[s]" to invite us out of such complacency and to help us overcome our blindnesses.[44] One of these "hard external[s]" involve the cries of the wounded—the voices that call out to us from their place of oppression, pain, and suffering.[45]

In due course, what turns out to be the result of listening to these cries and allowing them to lead us out of our own complacency? The answer to this question comes at the very end of "On a Certain Blindness in Human Beings." James's final paragraph reads:

> [W]hat is the result of all these considerations . . . ? It is nega-
> tive in one sense, but positive in another. It absolutely forbids
> us to be forward in pronouncing the meaninglessness of forms
> of existence other than our own; and it commands us to toler-
> ate, respect, and indulge those for whom we see harmlessly
> interested and happy in their own ways, however unintelligible
> these may be to us . . . [N]either the whole of truth nor the whole
> of good[ness] is revealed to any single observer, although each
> observer gains a partial superiority of insight from the peculiar
> position in which he stands . . . [When listening to the cries of the
> wounded, we learn that] prisons and sick-rooms have their spe-
> cial revelations. It is enough to ask of each of us that he should be
> faithful to his own opportunities and make the most of his own
> blessings, without presuming to regulate the rest of the . . . field.[46]

I insert the claim—when listening to the cries of the wounded, we learn that—as a way to make explicit the way James utilizes Royce's phrase. Those cries teach us something about goodness, about ourselves, about truth, about the world. Our vocation must include listening and responding to those cries.[47]

---

44. See W. James, "On a Certain Blindness in Human Beings," 119.

45. See W. James, "On a Certain Blindness in Human Beings," 119.

46. W. James, "On a Certain Blindness in Human Beings," 129.

47. I actually teach philosophy classes in the setting of a correctional facility. I call these students my incarcerated students as a way to distinguish them from my under-graduate students and to avoid referring to them as "prisoners." The word "prisoner" is no longer welcomed by those who are incarcerated, so I try not to use it. When people ask me why I teach at the correctional facility on a *pro bono* basis, I give a James-ean answer along the lines of: I might fulfill my vocation as a professor by teaching

In sum: in "The Moral Philosopher and the Moral Life," James connects the cries of the wounded with the vocation of the philosopher; in "On a Certain Blindness in Human Beings," James connects the cries of the wounded with vocation in general.

Contrasting James's and Royce's Uses of the Phrase

In his essay, entitled "The Cries of the Wounded," Roger Ward draws a strong contrast between James and Royce when it comes to their uses of the cries of the wounded. Ward sees three significant differences in their account of the cries of the wounded. First, James does not allow the cry of the philosopher to be a legitimate cry. Ward says, "James's notion of the moral life as satisfying 'alien demands' . . . is a clear dividing point" from Royce because "[f]or Royce, any perception of pain always includes our [the philosopher's] own."[48] For Royce, we understand the pain and suffering of others because of our own pain and suffering; for James, the cries that come from those who suffer remain alien to the philosopher: a philosopher's own pain and suffering does not help with understanding the pain and suffering of others.

Ward finds Royce close to Arthur Schopenhauer's view that the angst of the philosopher is what leads the philosopher to philosophizing in the first place.[49] Admittedly, I am torn on this point. On the one hand, my doctoral adviser—Peter Ochs—pounded in me the following argument as he prepared me to become a professor and scholar: "The philosopher's own suffering cannot . . . become the subject of philosophic concern."[50] Ochs's reasons are as follows (in my words, not Ochs's): "What philosophers perceive as their own suffering, and the remedy/remedies for that suffering cannot set norms for philosophical investigations. Suffering caused by problems within received traditions ought to be 'the subject of philosophic

---

undergraduate students on a daily basis, but my vocation meets a needed challenge when I spend time with my incarcerated students hearing about their wounds, listening to their cries, and teaching them philosophical arguments, ideas, and theories. Teaching them philosophy does not make their unintelligible lives intelligible on my standards; rather, teaching them philosophy means that they are treated as rational human beings for at least ninety minutes every week. They are wounded yet hopeful in our time together: they are wounded because of the unintelligibility of their daily lives and the de-humanization of our criminal justice system; yet, they become hopeful about themselves, their humanity, and their rational ability during our time together. Anecdotally, James certainly is right to suggest "prisons . . . have their special revelations."

48. Ward, "The Cries of the Wounded," 93.

49. See Ward, "The Cries of the Wounded," 93.

50. Ochs, *Peirce, Pragmatism, and the Logic of Scripture,* 297.

concern.'"[51] Paying attention to my own cries, according to Ochs, makes philosophy too individualistic. On the other hand, my own suffering has changed my mind on key philosophical questions as well as made me more sympathetic in thinking and writing.[52]

Second, Ward argues that James and Royce differ on what the response looks like to the cries of the wounded. Ward writes, "we see a divergence between Royce, for whom extending the moral insight [leads] to right thinking, and James, for whom the conditions of the cry prompts the individual philosopher to seek action."[53] Ward concludes that, for James, "peace is found only for the philosopher in allaying or answering demands."[54] On James's standards, listening to the cries of the wounded must lead to some action or set of actions that resolve the problems identified by those cries. This is part of James's philosophical position known as meliorism.[55] According to James, a philosopher cannot rest until such a resolution is reached. For Royce, listening to the cries of the wounded informs and shapes our thinking with the only promise of a resolution coming from God or the Absolute Knower. On this point, I find myself somewhere between James's and Royce's positions. On the one hand, I agree with Richard Rorty's argument that philosophers and professors are neither activists nor prophets.[56] On the other hand, my own thinking aligns more with Jürgen Habermas's argument that philosophers and professors ought to take part in

---

51. Goodson, "Peter Ochs and the Purpose of Philosophy," 99.

52. In *Keep Your Mind in Hell* (forthcoming from Cascade Books), for instance, I tell the story of how suffering a stroke changed the ways in which I view death and despair.

53. Ward, "The Cries of the Wounded," 94.

54. Ward, "The Cries of the Wounded," 94.

55. In *Pragmatism*, James defends his doctrine of meliorism on these terms: "It is clear that pragmatism must incline towards meliorism. Some conditions of the world's salvation are actually extant, and she cannot possibly close her eyes to this fact: and should the residual conditions come, salvation would become an accomplished reality . . . You may interpret the word 'salvation' in any way you like, and make it as diffuse and distributive, or as climacteric and integral a phenomenon as you please. Take, for example, any one of us in this room with the ideals which he cherishes, and is willing to live and work for. Every such ideal realized will be one moment in the world's salvation. But these particular ideals are not bare abstract possibilities. They are grounded, they are *live* possibilities, for we are their live champions and pledges, and if the complementary conditions come and add themselves, our ideals will become actual things. What now are the complementary conditions? They are first such a mixture of things as will in the fullness of time give us a chance, a gap that we can spring into, and, finally, *our act*. Does our act then *create* the world's salvation so far as it makes room for itself, so far as it leaps into the gap? Does it create, not the whole world's salvation of course, but just so much of this as itself covers of the world's extent?" (W. James, *Pragmatism*, 110).

56. See Rorty, "The Prophet and the Professor," 70–78.

communicative processes that seek resolutions in relation to the causes of suffering and woundedness.[57]

Third, Ward points out what might be considered the limitations or problems of James's nominalism. For Royce, we participate in external reality; we neither construct nor determine it. For James, we construct and determine external reality. In Ward's words: "the ground of James's postulate . . . from whom the philosopher receives the vocation of morality . . . [means] James remains in tension" with Royce in the sense "that we construct but do not receive the external reality of the world" for James.[58] In other words, James's identification of listening to the cries of the wounded as part and parcel of the vocation of the philosopher comes with no metaphysical backing or grounding because we do not respond to the external world, but we *make* what constitutes the external world as we go. Ward claims that James's reflections on vocation remain arbitrary and empty because they lack a metaphysical foundation.

Where do I stand in relation to James, Royce, and Ward on the cries of the wounded? I find that James has more of a "metaphysics" than Ward allows in his critique of James on vocation. Ultimately, I tend to side with James about the fact of irrationality within the world. James accepts that irrationality and unintelligibility will not be overcome, whereas Royce renders irrationality or unintelligibility an error in relation to the truths known by the Absolute Knower. In my view, *the messiness never gets completely cleaned up*. In this sense, I am thoroughly Jamesean when it comes to learning to live with irrationality and coming to recognize that I have my own irrational ways-of-being that others have to live with, as well. If listening to the cries of the wounded is part and parcel of one's vocation, what does it mean—according to James—that this aspect of our vocational lives should not come with the expectation of resolving the irrationality and messiness that causes the cries? To answer this question, we have to turn to James's *The Varieties of Religious Experience: A Study in Human Nature*.

Cries of the Wounded and Sick Souls

In his essay, "The Cries of the Wounded in *Pragmatism*," Sami Pihlström makes a bold and provocative claim concerning James's use of the phrase "cries of the wounded." According to Pihlström, "Only the sick soul really hears [the] cries."[59] In this subsection, I spell out how Pihlström arrives at

57. Goodson, *The Philosopher's Playground*, ch. 5.
58. Ward, "The Cries of the Wounded," 94.
59. Pihlström, "The Cries of the Wounded in *Pragmatism*," 313.

this bold and provocative claim and eventually offer my own reflections on the connection between the cries of the wounded and James's category of the sick soul found in his most famous work, *The Varieties of Religious Experience: A Study in Human Nature*. While I agree with most of Pihlström's reading of James, in the next subsection I make two claims that differ slightly from Pihlström's thesis: first, I reverse Pihlström's ordering in the sense that *listening to the cries of the wounded turns one into a sick soul*; second, I seek to connect the cries of the wounded with both sick souls *and* divided selves.

Pihlström interweaves three writings of James's: "The Moral Philosopher and the Moral Life" (1891), *The Varieties of Religious Experience* (1902), and *Pragmatism* (1907). How does he arrive at the conclusion that only "the sick soul really [hears] cries" by interweaving these three texts?[60] He arrives there by starting in 1907, jumping back to 1891, and then landing in 1902.

About James's argument in *Pragmatism*, Pihlström claims that James's pragmatism ought to be understood as

> a method that looks into the possible futures of the world in which we live, focusing on what the different metaphysical views "promise" and on whether they can function as philosophies of hope, especially from the point of view of the "wounded," the sufferers or the victims of evil. This is a profoundly ethical undertaking. Far from maintaining that our metaphysical problems ought to be solved first—or that we could simply get rid of them—in order to turn to ethical problems later, James is suggesting that we should begin our metaphysical inquiries from the ethical examination of the practical relevance of the rival metaphysical ideas that have been or can be proposed, and that this ethical examination can only take place if we focus on how "the wounded" would respond to this or that world-picture being true.[61]

So, Pihlström first premise: James writes *Pragmatism* in order to come up with a philosophical method that tests out metaphysical arguments and theories based upon the ethical question, how would "'the wounded' . . . respond to this or that world-picture being true"?[62] With this premise, Pihlström offers an interpretation of and orientation toward *Pragmatism* on the terms of "The Moral Philosopher and the Moral Life."

Does Pihlström have textual evidence for this peculiar reading of *Pragmatism*? Yes, he does. He offers two pieces of evidence—one conceptual and one concrete—and both found in the first lecture of *Pragmatism*.

60. See Pihlström, "The Cries of the Wounded in *Pragmatism*," 313.

61. Pihlström, "The Cries of the Wounded in *Pragmatism*," 298.

62. See Pihlström, "The Cries of the Wounded in *Pragmatism*," 298.

Conceptually, James tells his readers (without him explicitly using the language of cries or the wounded) that pragmatists refuse "to be deaf to the cries of the wounded."[63] This claim gets "presented as one of the ethical motivations grounding the entire pragmatist method in [James's] first lecture of *Pragmatism*."[64] Concretely, James refers "to the actual fate of some extremely unhappy individuals, such as . . . an unemployed . . . , disappointed[,] and discouraged sick man who found his family lacking food and eventually committed suicide."[65] While James does not use the phrase "cries of the wounded" in *Pragmatism*, he gives concrete examples of what those cries look like from actual wounded people.

Second, Pihlström employs two phrases (healthy-mindedness and sick soul) from *The Varieties of Religious Experience* to introduce James's approach to the problem of evil. He writes,

> Ethics in general, and evil in particular—as a frame of ethics, as urging us into adopting the moral perspective, as "hurting us into morality"—is a compelling issue for the "sick soul" rather than the "healthy-minded." . . . [T]o adopt a truly ethical attitude to the cries of the wounded is to embrace a fundamentally *melancholic* view of the world. The problem of evil . . . emerges as a "transcendental" frame, a transcultural . . . condition making ethical seriousness possible.[66]

Pihlström's second premise introduces the connection between James's understanding of the sick soul in *The Varieties of Religious Experience* with the claim that listening to the cries of the wounded requires "a fundamentally *melancholic* view of the world."[67] According to James, having a melancholic view of the world becomes one of the primary attributes of what it means to be a sick soul. With this premise, Pihlström establishes a connection between the phrases cries of the wounded and sick soul.

Third, Pihlström draws a more specific contrast between the healthy-minded and the sick soul in relation to the cries of the wounded as well as to the problem of evil. He claims that James's

---

63. Pihlström, "The Cries of the Wounded in *Pragmatism*," 305.

64. Pihlström, "The Cries of the Wounded in *Pragmatism*," 305.

65. Pihlström, "The Cries of the Wounded in *Pragmatism*," 305. Pihlström points out that James uses these concrete examples in order to contrast his method from "the airy and shallow optimism of current religious philosoph[ies]." James has Royce in mind as his target here.

66. Pihlström, "The Cries of the Wounded in *Pragmatism*," 299. Note Pihlström's Kantian interpretation of James: "The problem of evil . . . emerges as a 'transcendental' frame, a transcultural . . . condition making ethical seriousness possible."

67. Pihlström, "The Cries of the Wounded in *Pragmatism*," 299.

> pragmatism is primarily a philosophy *not* for the "healthy-minded" person who "deliberately excludes evil from [her or his] field of vision." . . . but for the "sick soul" who views evil as the very essence of life and of the world . . . While the *Varieties* speaks about the sick soul, *Pragmatism* urges us to take seriously the "lost-soul" and the "damned soul." . . . To do so is to hear, or at least try to hear, the cries of the wounded—and to refuse . . . the bargain of purchasing the happiness of millions with the price of the eternal torment of a single "lost soul."[68]

Who are the wounded? Those who are damned; those who are lost. The sick soul, developed and discussed in *The Varieties of Religious Experience*, has the ability "to take seriously the 'lost soul' and the 'damned soul.'"[69] In addition to having a "*melancholic* view of the world," the sick soul can hear the cries of the wounded because they relate best to the damned and to the lost.[70]

Pihlström's final premise returns to the method developed by James in *Pragmatism*. According to Pihlström,

> [The] fight against evil . . . is part and parcel of the pragmatic method itself, as [James] developed in *Pragmatism*. It is by employing this method that we turn our attention to ethics whenever we are concerned with the world in any allegedly or apparently non-ethical sense—conceptually, metaphysically, or perhaps religiously—and it is through that kind of reflective attention that we inquire into what needs to be done by listening, as carefully as we can, to the cries of the wounded.[71]

James's method requires philosophers, scholars, and thinkers—who have a "kind of reflective attention"—to listen "as carefully as [they] can, to the cries of the wounded."[72]

This argument leads directly to the bold and provocative claim: "*Only* the sick soul really hears [the] cries."[73] Pihlström does not back off in any way from this bold and provocative claim: "*Only* the sick soul really hears [the] cries."[74] He does, however, both broaden and clarify the claim with

---

68. Pihlström, "The Cries of the Wounded in *Pragmatism*," 306.

69. Pihlström, "The Cries of the Wounded in *Pragmatism*," 306.

70. See Pihlström, "The Cries of the Wounded in *Pragmatism*," 306.

71. Pihlström, "The Cries of the Wounded in *Pragmatism*," 313.

72. Pihlström, "The Cries of the Wounded in *Pragmatism*," 313.

73. Pihlström, "The Cries of the Wounded in *Pragmatism*," 313; emphasis added.

74. Pihlström, "The Cries of the Wounded in *Pragmatism*," 313; emphasis added.

this conclusion: "The pragmatist ethical thinker *is* . . . a sick soul in this (transcendental) sense."[75]

In summary, there are two aspects of Pihlström's interpretation of James worth highlighting in relation to the purposes and questions of the present chapter. First, Pihlström connects the phrase "cries of the wounded" with James's understanding of sick souls in *The Varieties of Religious Experience*. Second, Pihlström offers a Kantian transcendentalist interpretation of James by teasing out the epistemological conditions necessary for being able to hear the cries of the wounded. I agree with Pihlström that the language of cries becomes the way that pragmatists understand what we mean by the wounded world, but where do I disagree with his account?

Cries of the Wounded, Divided Selves, and Sick Souls

In James's *The Varieties of Religious Experience*, divided self, healthy-mindedness, and sick soul come to us as three consecutive chapters or lectures. In my judgment, these lectures are James's best in terms of fulfilling the promissory note of the subtitle of *The Varieties of Religious Experience: A Study in Human Nature*. Working through James's three categories teaches us, I believe, that listening to the cries of the wounded leads one to becoming either a divided self or a sick soul (this represents my disagreement with Pihlström).

At the outset, James seeks to limit his judgments about or against those who are healthy-minded.[76] Ultimately, however, he cannot help but make negative moral judgments against them when he contrasts the healthy-minded from those who are sick souls:

> The method of averting one's attention from evil, and living simply in the light of good is splendid as long as it will work. It will work with many persons; it will work far more generally than most of us are ready to suppose; and within the sphere of its successful operation there is nothing to be said against it as a religious solution. But it breaks down impotently as soon as melancholy comes; and even though one can be quite free from melancholy one's self [*sic*], there is no doubt that healthy-mindedness is inadequate as a philosophical doctrine, because the evil facts which it refuses positively to account for are a genuine portion of reality; and they may after all be the best key to life's

75. Pihlström, "The Cries of the Wounded in *Pragmatism*," 313; emphasis added.

76. "I am not yet pretending finally to judge any of these attitudes, I am only describing their variety" (James, *The Varieties of Religious Experience*, 126).

significance, and possibly the only openers of our eyes to the deepest levels of truth.[77]

The healthy-minded remain healthy-minded because they neither hear nor listen for the cries of the wounded.

I argue that those who come to constantly hear the cries of the wounded become sick souls in the sense that they come to know "deepest levels of truth."[78] To identify the brokenness and woundedness of the world eventually turns one into a sick soul. To gain awareness of the multiple cries being expressed in a wounded world leads to becoming a sick soul about the world. Based on James's meliorism, I argue additionally that listening to the cries of the wounded means that the sick soul takes some action or set of actions that resolve the problems identified by those cries.

Or, perhaps, listening to the cries of the wounded leads to becoming a divided self? In *The Varieties of Religious Experience*, James says that a divided self is someone for whom

> [t]he higher and the lower feelings, the useful and the erring impulses, begin by being a comparative chaos within us—they must end by forming a stable system of functions in right subordination. Unhappiness is apt to characterize the period of order-making and struggle. If the individual be of tender conscience and religiously quickened, the unhappiness will take the form of moral remorse and compunction, of feeling inwardly vile and wrong, and of standing in false relations to [God].[79]

Very different from Royce's Absolute Knower, this is where James brings God into the picture. For James, a divided self is one who finds themself "standing in false relations to [God]."[80] What makes the divided self a divided self is that they accept and embrace the cognitive dissonance that comes with hearing the cries of the wounded but continue practices that cause and contribute to such suffering. A divided self hears the cries of the wounded, but does not know how to behave differently in relation to those cries. This is why they feel "inwardly vile and wrong."[81]

Instead of claiming that the sick soul is the disposition required for hearing the cries of the wounded, I argue that listening to the cries of the wounded eventually turns one into either a divided self or a sick soul.

77. James, *The Varieties of Religious Experience*, 140.

78. James, *The Varieties of Religious Experience*, 140.

79. James, *The Varieties of Religious Experience*, 146.

80. James, *The Varieties of Religious Experience*, 146.

81. James, *The Varieties of Religious Experience*, 146.

Listening to the cries of the wounded leads to becoming a divided self or a sick soul: a divided self does not know how to change their own behavior in relation to the cries they hear, whereas a sick soul thinks more melioristically—that is, takes some action or set of actions that resolve the problems identified by those cries.

CONCLUSION: CRIES OF THE WOUNDED IN CONTEMPORARY PRAGMATISM

Within contemporary pragmatism, three original thinkers and well-known pragmatists (Hilary Putnam, Charlene Haddock Seigfried, and Cornel West) employ the language of the cries of the wounded. Interestingly, two of them (Putnam and Seigfried) credit William James—not Josiah Royce—with the phrase. As a conclusion to this chapter, I briefly explore how Putnam, Seigfried, and West use the phrase "cries of the wounded."

In *The Collapse of the Fact/Value Dichotomy*, which is one of his few books on ethics, the American pragmatist and former Harvard professor Hilary Putnam (now of blessed memory) quotes William James's use of "cries of the wounded" on two occasions. First, in order to critique the moral reasoning of German philosopher Jürgen Habermas—who Putnam considers as more of an idealist than a pragmatist—Putnam writes:

> For a discussion to be ideal in the Habermasian sense it is not enough that those who do the arguing obey the principles of discourse ethics in their arguments *with one another*; even those who do not speak up must be regarded as members of the group (otherwise it does not include all affected persons), and every member of the group must have a non-manipulative attitude towards every other [member]. With respect to those who are unable to argue well, there is always William James's beautiful demand that we "listen to the cries of the wounded." One does not have to be articulate to cry out! If the cries of the wounded are ignored, then the speech situation is certainly not "ideal" in a Habermasian . . . sense.[82]

In this passage, Putnam utilizes the phrase "cries of the wounded" as what we should listen for in regards to "those who are unable to argue well."[83] In Putnam's words, "One does not have to be articulate to cry out!"[84] Ignoring

82. Putnam, *The Collapse of the Fact/Value Dichotomy*, 130.
83. Putnam, *The Collapse of the Fact/Value Dichotomy*, 130.
84. Putnam, *The Collapse of the Fact/Value Dichotomy*, 130.

such cries is what Putnam deems as the problem; the problem is not the lack of articulation from those who cry out. I agree with Putnam's insight about how a cry can serve as a kind of communicative action for "those . . . unable to argue well," but I disagree with Putnam that Habermas's theory of communicative action does not allow for this (a point I only assert here and do not fully defend).

Second, Putnam uses the phrase in order to critique the French philosopher Jean-Francois Lyotard's postmodernism. Putnam writes:

> It is very likely that what he [Lyotard] envisaged was the possibility of a discussion in which those who are articulate do have a good will towards the inarticulate, at least subjectively, and do hear at least the most obvious "cries of the wounded." But one can have good will, at least subjectively, and systematically misinterpret those cries, and do so in one's own interest.[85]

According to Putnam, Lyotard's faith in the "good will" of humanity does not necessarily lead to the ability to properly listen to the cries of the wounded.[86] Echoing Royce's problem with selfishness (although Putnam does not acknowledge this point of similarity), Putnam suggests that we need to get past our own self-interest in order to properly listen to the cries of the wounded.

In *Pragmatism and Feminism*, Charlene Haddock Seigfried uses the phrase to affirm and suggest human societal progress. Seigfried claims:

> [T]he criterion James gives for identifying mistaken moral choices should awaken curiosity about the possibility of appropriating his ethical outlook. He says that when we make a bad mistake "the cries of the wounded will soon inform us of the fact" . . . Thanks to recent advances in feminist and postcolonial achievements and scholarship, such cries are finally beginning to be heard.[87]

According to Seigfried, both feminism and postcolonialism have achieved listening to the cries of the wounded. In this way, Seigfried seems to affirm that certain parts of and particular people in society have followed James's account of vocation on the terms of learning to listen to the cries of the wounded. Of course, more work still needs to be accomplished. In other words, affirming that more cries are being heard should not be used to continue our blindness toward those who still experience oppression and suffering.

---

85. Putnam, *The Collapse of the Fact/Value Dichotomy*, 130.

86. See Putnam, *The Collapse of the Fact/Value Dichotomy*, 130.

87. Seigfried, *Pragmatism and Feminism*, 223.

Although he does not explicitly use the phrase "cries of the wounded," Cornel West connects the language of cries in the Hebrew Prophets with his own version of pragmatism—known as prophetic pragmatism. In *Introducing Prophetic Pragmatism*, I explain West's connection between cries and his version of pragmatism in the following way:

> Toward the end of *Democracy Matters*, West . . . develops the language and logic of the Hebrew Prophets—answering specific questions. What is the initial impetus for prophetic reasoning? According to West, "The Jewish invention of the prophetic begins with the cries for help and tears of sorrow of an oppressed people." What is the specific language involved with prophetic reasoning? West redirects this question to the language heard by the Hebrew Prophets: "The premier prophetic language is the language of cries and tears because human hurt and misery give rise to visions of justice and deeds of compassion." Does prophetic reasoning stop with this "language of cries and tears"? West says not at all: "For the prophetic tradition, the cries and tears of an oppressed people signify an alternative to oppression and symbolize an allegiance to a God who requires human deeds that address these cries and tears." Prophetic reasoning involves a theo-logic of loyalty to God through good deeds and human actions addressing the "cries and tears." This logic of loyalty comes with a logic of righteousness as well; what is this logic? West claims, "The prophetic tradition is fueled by a righteous indignation at injustice—a moral urgency to address the cries and tears of oppressed peoples." This logic of "righteous indignation" leads to a specific way of life that has three characteristics. For West, "The prophetic tradition is an infectious and invigorating way of life and struggle"—which (a) "generates the courage to care and act . . . ," (b) "awakens us from the fashionable ways of being indifferent to other people's suffering . . . ," and (c) "unleashes ethical energy and political engagement that explodes all forms of our egocentric predicaments and tribalistic mind-sets." This offers us an important account of the language and logic of the Hebrew Prophets within West's prophetic pragmatism.[88]

West sees in the language of cries a strong call for "a righteous indignation at injustice" and a "moral urgency" to respond to those who experience oppression and suffering.[89] It would not be too much to infer that West's pro-

---

88. Goodson and Stone, *Introducing Prophetic Pragmatism*, 64.

89. See West, *Democracy Matters*, 215.

phetic pragmatism is driven by a serious and sobering call to better listen to and respond to the cries of the wounded. Again (and finally), the language of cries—whether from the Hebrew Prophets, from Josiah Royce's absolute idealism, or William James's pragmatism—becomes the way to understand the wounded world within American philosophy. In the next chapter, Brad Elliott Stone continues this discussion and goes deeper into Cornel West's prophetic pragmatism.

2

Prophetic Pragmatism and the Tragic Sense of Life

Brad Elliott Stone

IN 1993, THE SAME year as the publication of *Race Matters*, Cornel West published *Keeping Faith: Philosophy and Race in America*. Consisting mostly of previous published essays from 1982 to 1993, the anthology includes two new pieces: the preface, "The Difficulty of Keeping Faith," and the essay, "Pragmatism and the Sense of the Tragic." The latter essay is described in its entry in *The Cornel West Reader* as "part of a book on Josiah Royce" that remains unfinished.[1] This chapter offers a reading of this often neglected but important essay by West.

My reading moves between West's essay and other works referenced within it. One such work is Sidney Hook's 1959 presidential address to the American Philosophical Association (APA), titled "Pragmatism and the Tragic Sense of Life." In that address, Hook investigates the need for philosophers to not lose sight of what motivates people to seek philosophical answers to fundamental questions. In what can be best described as a final plea for America to strengthen its pragmatist philosophical footing in light

---

1. West, *The Cornel West Reader*, 174.

37

of the rise of analytic philosophy in the United States, Hook highlights "the saving message" that philosophy can give.[2]

Among the figures mentioned by Hook is the Spanish philosopher Miguel de Unamuno, whose 1912 *Tragic Sense of Life* played a role in Hook's title. Although Hook does not go into any significant details about Unamuno's understanding of the term, reducing Unamuno's position to "the hysterical lament that man is not immortal,"[3] Hook's account of pragmatism in light of life's tragic sense is actually closer to Unamuno's actual argument: philosophy, once divorced from the concrete experience and problems that humans face, runs the risk of irrelevance. This is what gives Hook's address its urgency. Although West never wrote anything on Unamuno, West points out in "The Making of an American Radical Democrat of African Descent" that Unamuno was one of the thinkers he kept "close to [his] heart" while studying at Princeton.[4] By exploring Unamuno's notion of the tragic sense of life, we will better understand the appeal of the tragic (and the tragicomic) in West's works.

The central figure of West's essay is Royce. West claims that Royce is the only American philosopher who comes close to properly analyzing the role of the tragic. The essay claims that Royce's pragmatism complements and completes Dewey's pragmatism, combining to form the philosophical framework that brings about the visions of Jefferson, Emerson, and Lincoln (who serve as the triumvirate of American democracy that frames West's discussion). Dewey correctly addresses the Jeffersonian and Emersonian dimensions of democracy, but fails to account for the unique Lincolnian dimension: tragedy. Royce, influenced by Schopenhauer, addresses all three, but is compromised by his insistence on idealism. I will address the problem of idealism in chapter 5.

West's prophetic pragmatism fulfills the insight of Royce by addressing the problem of evil as it pertains to the African American experience. Using the insights of Hook, Unamuno, and Royce, among others, West offers a tragicomic philosophical sensibility that indeed can respond to the tragic sense of life.

2. Hook, "Pragmatism and the Tragic Sense of Life," 6.

3. Hook, "Pragmatism and the Tragic Sense of Life," 10.

4. West, *The Cornel West Reader*, 7.

SIDNEY HOOK ON PRAGMATISM AND
THE TRAGIC SENSE OF LIFE

Hook's APA presidential address highlights the need for and purpose of philosophy at a time when philosophers' relevance in the American life was beginning to wane. Although it is true that philosophy is the love and pursuit of wisdom, the rising tendency is for philosophy (namely, philosophers) to stand aloof, clarifying ideas about issues with which no one is actually struggling. Hook seeks to refocus philosophy towards real wisdom: the philosopher's quest for wisdom and understanding should lead one to "immerse [one]self in the actual subject matters . . . out of which life's problems arise."[5] To be fair, it is not the philosopher's task to solve life's problems; however, the philosopher is to play a key role in thinking through those problems, and the ideas generated ought to clarify, illuminate, and inspire action. Hook emphasizes that philosophy is not a "quest for salvation" but rather "a pursuit of understanding . . . issues and their possible upshot."[6] Even metaphysics, whose theoretical nature can suggest disengaged reflection on the nature of inert reality, has practical implications. Hook defines metaphysics as "a description of those gross features of the world which constitute the backdrop of the theatre of human activity against which [people] play out their lives."[7] All pragmatist philosophy, regardless of subfield, seeks to aid human activity.

In this address, Hook focuses on the tragic sense of life as a feature of the world, which indeed serves as a backdrop to human activity, as a theme people face and with which they will have to deal. This tragic sense of life is revealed to us phenomenologically "in the defeat of plans and hopes."[8] What, however, is the nature of the tragic?

Hook begins by excluding death as the main element of the tragic. Life is not tragic because we are mortal. This fact, Hook argues, is "certainly unworthy of any philosophy which conceives itself as a quest for wisdom."[9] After all, no amount of human activity can undo the fact that human beings die. In this sense, death produces meaning: death gives life meaning and urgency. The tragic takes place inside of life. The human struggle takes place inside of one's life. The tragic finds itself "in a contingent world of finite men, vulnerable to powers they cannot control which sometimes robs them

---

5. Hook, "Pragmatism and the Tragic Sense of Life," 8.
6. Hook, "Pragmatism and the Tragic Sense of Life," 9.
7. Hook, "Pragmatism and the Tragic Sense of Life," 10.
8. Hook, "Pragmatism and the Tragic Sense of Life," 11.
9. Hook, "Pragmatism and the Tragic Sense of Life," 12.

of the possibility of any justifying consummations."[10] Death is actually the end of one's tragic existence, as it were. Hence the phrase "the tragic sense *of life*"; the tragic is about life—the very lives that we live. Hook concludes the discussion of death by noting that "[i]t would be truer to call tragic a world in which [people] wanted to die but couldn't."[11] In that case, the plan and hope for death would be defeated, which is precisely Hook's definition of the tragic. It is not physical pain and suffering nor death that defines the tragic; rather, it is the frustration of plans and hopes. People are willing to experience pain to fulfill their goal. One can endure suffering if it is clear that on the other side of that suffering one will get what one desires. Pain and suffering would be tragic only in such cases when, for all of that pain and suffering, the desired outcome did not occur.

Having eliminated mere mortality from his definition of tragedy, Hook defines the tragic as a moral phenomenon "rooted in the very nature of the moral experience and the phenomenon of moral choice."[12] As a matter of morality, Hook outlines three instances of the tragic: the conflict of competing goods, the conflict between the good and the right, and the conflict of competing rights. In the first case, choosing one good sacrifices or delays some other good. Of course, the competing goods of interest to Hook are goods that are "consequential for the future."[13] The moral choices are tragic because each of the competing goods are indeed consequential. This view does not require one to be a consequentialist, where one is to maximize the good for the greatest number of people; rather, it is the simple acknowledgment that pursuing one good costs us an equally preferable good. The tragic comes from recognizing that not every good can be simultaneously performed or realized.

The conflicts between the right and the good are commonplace moral quandaries. From Kant to W. D. Ross, moral philosophers have had to worry about right actions that have evil consequences and pursuits of good that violate *prima facie* moral duties. Often the good and the right work harmoniously, but when they do not, one finds oneself in a tragic situation. This tragic conflict of the right and the good is inevitable and is not easily resolved. When genuinely confronted with a conflict between the good and the right, one of the two prevails, costing us the other (even if only momentarily). As Hook states, "[n]o matter how we choose, we must either betray the ideal of the greater good or the ideal of right or justice. In this lies the agony of the

---

10. Hook, "Pragmatism and the Tragic Sense of Life," 12.
11. Hook, "Pragmatism and the Tragic Sense of Life," 13.
12. Hook, "Pragmatism and the Tragic Sense of Life," 13.
13. Hook, "Pragmatism and the Tragic Sense of Life," 14.

choice."[14] We always choose injustice in the name of a greater good or we justify a particular diminishment of good by appeals to justice. Either way, there is a cost. The tragic sense of life is that we must always pay that cost.

The third instance of the tragic, which Hook considers to be "the most dramatic of all moral conflicts,"[15] is the fact that there are conflicts between competing rights (laws, notions of justice, etc.). Arguing against Ross, Hook does not believe that one could have a prioritization of one's *prima facie* duties that would resolve the tragic dimension of the conflict of duties. Such moral intuitionism merely explains why one fulfilled one duty at the expense of other duties. It would not provide moral justification; it merely explains one's choice. The tragic is in the fact that one must fulfill one duty at the expense of the others. At best we simply try to do the best we can, paying the tragic cost for all choices we make in such instances.

The example Hook gives in his discussion of the conflict between competing rights is very appropriate given the context of this chapter's discussion of tragedy and racial justice. Hook discusses—in 1959, although we still grapple with this issue today—the moral problem of reparations for past injustices:

> Irony is compounded with tragedy in the fact that many of the rights we presently enjoy we owe to our ancestors who in the process of winning them for us deprived others of their rights ... Yet as a rule it would be a new injustice to seek to redress the original injustice by depriving those of their possessions who hold present title to them. Every just demand for reparations ... is an unjust demand on the descendants of its citizens who ... were not responsible for the deeds of aggression.[16]

Notice that Hook considers the demand for reparations to be a just demand. The right to keep one's possessions that they themselves personally did not unjustly gain (of course, this is the point of contention) is also just. Of course, each side of the issue will claim injustice. This is why the US legacy of slavery is truly tragic; the rectification of past injustices includes a present injustice. The choice about reparations will be unable to avoid this conflict of rights.

The choice between two competing rights is tragic because the conflict of rights itself cannot and does not paralyze choice. One must choose one justice that causes injustice to occur. The historical weight of the example of reparations does not add to the tragic sense of moral choice in terms of conflicting rights; all such choices are, for Hook, tragic.

14. Hook, "Pragmatism and the Tragic Sense of Life," 16.
15. Hook, "Pragmatism and the Tragic Sense of Life," 17.
16. Hook, "Pragmatism and the Tragic Sense of Life," 18.

Hook finishes his essay by considering three approaches to facing the tragic sense of life: history, love, and creative intelligence (pragmatism). The first two approaches are swiftly dismissed. Hook argues that history "tries to put a gloss of reason over the terrible events which constitute so much of the historical process."[17] This "gloss of reason" rationalizes the decisions that were made, as if the outcome of past decisions could ever justify the decision made, removing from those past choices their own tragic dimension. Hook sees such use of history as a type of theodicy, a way of evading or alleviating tragedy through a notion of necessity. In reality, history provides a kind of *post hoc ergo propter hoc* fallacious response to the tragic sense of life. From the same past decisions, different presents were equally possible, so our current present is influenced by the past but is not connected by necessity to it in the way history suggests. To be fair, contemporary historians have become more cognizant of this temptation.

Love is useful for forgiving the consequences of decisions made, but it is not very useful at the tragic moment of choice. One could say that we erroneously ascribe tragedy to the consequences of decisions instead of recognizing that the tragedy is in the moments of decision themselves, regardless of the consequences. Thus, Hook argues, love "is no guide to social conflict" and "has no bearing whatever for the organization of any human society."[18] If love appears in the tragic, it would be either as a good or as a duty, and thus would be an ingredient in one of the three forms of the tragic. Hence, love *per se* is not an acceptable approach for dealing with the tragic sense of life.

Creative intelligence, in contrast to history and love, acknowledges the tragic sense of life head-on. It "tries to make it possible for [people] to live with the tragic conflict of goods and rights and duties . . . through informed and responsible decision."[19] Pragmatism, the philosophical attitude endorsed by Hook, "doesn't resign itself to the bare fact of tragedy or take easy ways out."[20] Since all moral decisions are tragic, we must come to terms with that fact. Pragmatism thinks through the costs of decisions, the consequences of thinking, and the clarity of ideas so as "to reduce the costs of tragedy."[21] This, Hook claims, is why pragmatism prefers meliorism over optimism: optimists miscalculate costs, ignore obvious possible consequences, and simply "hope for the best." Pragmatists know better, fully

---

17. Hook, "Pragmatism and the Tragic Sense of Life," 18.
18. Hook, "Pragmatism and the Tragic Sense of Life," 19.
19. Hook, "Pragmatism and the Tragic Sense of Life," 19.
20. Hook, "Pragmatism and the Tragic Sense of Life," 20.
21. Hook, "Pragmatism and the Tragic Sense of Life," 23.

aware that every idea, every thought, every choice, and every action has consequences that usually conflict with the consequences of other ideas, thoughts, choices, and actions. Thus, one must think through choices in informed ways with the hope of minimizing costs and thus minimizing tragedy. In this sense, meliorism is not simply a hope for a better tomorrow—it is the full awareness that a better tomorrow has a cost that needs to be paid today at hopefully the lowest possible price. One cannot remove the tragic, so pragmatism's goal is to improve our ability to perform this tragic activity called life.

Yet, as Hook reminds us, "[t]here is more in life than the sense of the tragic. There is laughter and joy and the sustaining discipline of work . . . There are other uses for intelligence besides the resolution of human difficulties."[22] Not everything is tragic, but we must deal with the tragedy there is. Pragmatism seeks to correctly deal with the tragic and the joyous—what West correctly combines in his notion of the tragicomic. Our commitment is to "enlarging human freedom in a precarious and tragic world by the arts of intelligent social control."[23] Any philosophical position that fails to account for a precarious and tragic world will ultimately be unsatisfying.

UNAMUNO ON THE TRAGIC SENSE OF LIFE AND THE TRAGICOMIC SPANISH SPIRIT

Although he uses Unamuno's title *Tragic Sense of Life* in the title of his own address, Hook does not go into any significant detail about Unamuno's arguments. Upon introducing the phrase "the tragic sense of life" in the address, Hook says the following:

> The juxtaposition of the expression "pragmatism" and "the tragic sense of life" may appear bewildering to those who understand pragmatism as a narrow theory of meaning and "the tragic sense of life" as the hysterical lament that man is not immortal—the theme song of Unamuno's book of that title.[24]

Hook's description of Unamuno here is unfortunate. Although Unamuno considers it tragic that one is unable to know whether there is an afterlife (and thus does not know whether there is a purpose in holding particular religious views by faith or attempting to prove the existence of God by

22. Hook, "Pragmatism and the Tragic Sense of Life," 26.
23. Hook, "Pragmatism and the Tragic Sense of Life," 26.
24. Hook, "Pragmatism and the Tragic Sense of Life," 10.

means of natural theology), it is incorrect to say that the question is "the theme song" of the whole book.

Later on, when Hook is discussing creative intelligence, contrasting it with history and love, he returns to Unamuno:

> Contrast this attitude towards tragedy with the Hegelian fetish-ism of history which in the end is but the rationalization of cruelty. Contrast it with the Judaic-Christian conception which offers at the price of truth, the hope that the felicities of salvation will both explain and recompense human suffering. Contrast that with the attitude of Unamuno whose hunger for immortal-ity is so intense that he sees in intelligence or reason the chief enemy of life, both in time and eternity. For him the joy and de-light of life is the conflict of value and value no matter what the cost. "The very essence of tragedy," he tells us, "is the combat of life with reason." And since the Inquisitor is concerned with the eternal life of his victim's soul, the potential victim must defend the Inquisitor's place in society and regard him as far superior to the merchant who merely ministers to his needs. "There is much more humanity in the Inquisitor," he says. Crazed by his thirst for the infinite, Unamuno glorifies war as the best means of spread-ing love and knowledge. He illustrates the dialectic of total ab-surdity and caprice in thought which often prepares the way for atrocity in life. Here is no quest for the better, for the extension of reasonable controls in life and society, for peace in action.[25]

Again, the critique is unfortunate. Hook presents Unamuno here as a fideist who cannot come to terms with himself as a finite mortal and is willing to glorify war as a way of spreading love and knowledge.

Meanwhile, a majority of *Tragic Sense of Life* affirms Hook's claims about the role of philosophy and the need for philosophy to be directly con-nected to the concerns of human beings. Unamuno, after all, was a reader of James (and refers to James by name at several moments in the book). Thus, the connection between pragmatism and Unamuno was not as far of a stretch as Hook presented it to be.

Why defend Unamuno against Hook here? One reason is personal, the other philosophical. Unamuno's *Tragic Sense of Life* has a central place in my formation as a philosopher. Like many Spanish philosophers, Unamuno's writings are not studied much in the United States. I came to Unamuno's work by studying Spanish with Charles Seabrook at Georgetown College. Under his guidance, along with my philosophy professor and mentor,

---

25. Hook, "Pragmatism and the Tragic Sense of Life," 21.

Norman Wirzba, I wrote my undergraduate honors thesis on Unamuno and Kierkegaard. I then won a Fulbright Scholarship to independently study Unamuno at the Casa-Museo Unamuno at the University of Salamanca. More important to this chapter is that Unamuno highlights the tragicomic that emerges from the tragic sense of life, a theme that West, reader of Unamuno himself, develops in the sections that follow.

The central theme of Unamuno's book is that philosophical efforts that are divorced from the concrete conditions of human life lead us astray and even fight against those concrete conditions. On the one hand, there is what Unamuno calls "the man of flesh and bone" (*el hombre de carne y hueso*); on the other hand, there is "the human being," the "no-man," the philosophical abstract shell of the human person that has unfortunately served as the object of philosophical inquiry. As Unamuno states, "this concrete man, this man of flesh and bone, is at once the subject and the supreme object of all philosophy, whether certain self-styled philosophers like it or not."[26] Unamuno defines the man of flesh and bone as "the man who is born, suffers, and dies—above all, who dies."[27] Whereas Hook treats this as a lament, I see Unamuno as honest about the role of mortality in the meaning of being human, anticipating Heidegger's understanding of human existence in terms of being-towards-death.

Unamuno argues that philosophy has not held the man of flesh and bone as the starting point, instead understanding human beings as "the rational animals." No surprise, then, God is determined by the philosophers merely as a first cause, prime mover, and creator. Unamuno argues that insofar as human beings are conscious not only of the world but of their own mortal existence, human desire is often at odds with the interests pursued by philosophy. For example, humans are finite, but philosophy proceeds *sub specie aeternitatis*. Why should philosophy seek eternal truths, infinite knowledge, etc., if we, people of flesh and bone, are mortal? What could philosophy say about how to live a mortal, finite life if it does not address our finite longings?

The longings in question, "the only real vital problem," relate to "the problem of our individual and personal destiny, of the immortality of the soul."[28] This is the origin of the tragic sense of life: not that we are not immortal, but that we seek immortality even though we are mortal. Philosophy and religion are both examples, according to Unamuno, of efforts to move from mortality to immortality. Thus the tragic sense of life is found in the fact

---

26. Unamuno, *Tragic Sense of Life*, 1–2.

27. Unamuno, *Tragic Sense of Life*, 1.

28. Unamuno, *Tragic Sense of Life*, 4.

that we fully acknowledge our mortality while trying to be eternal. In this sense, Unamuno is close to Kierkegaard's notion of despair in *Sickness Unto Death*: we despair because we are finite yet have an idea of the eternal (even about our own being). Philosophy and religion move this eternity to either a Platonic realm of perfect ideas or an afterlife governed by an eternal God.

To be sure, Unamuno's writing style is not for professional philosophers. Unamuno wrote the essays that compose *Tragic Sense of Life* as monthly entries for a public intellectual journal, so the audience is the general public. In these essays, he is trying to explain why early twentieth-century Spaniards are feeling despair, as the end of the Spanish Empire will lead to Spain becoming more properly "European" (which Unamuno defines strictly in terms of France and Germany). With most European philosophy being Protestant in nature and intention, will the Spanish Catholic spirit be lost, dissolved by "reason"? Unamuno is not against intelligence or reason in general: he is referring to a particular Cartesian project, perfected by Kant and Hegel, that ridicules many of the ideas that Spaniards hold. If "reason" will challenge so much of Spanish culture, perhaps one needs to declare war against "reason." As Unamuno asserts, his view is not "irrational," contrary to "reason"; it is "contra-rational," against "reason." Unamuno calls his view "faith." Framing the issue in these terms is indeed unfortunate, for it allows Hook to see Unamuno's position merely as a faith vs. reason debate, when Unamuno is actually arguing for the opposite; anything that should count as philosophical reasoning must be of use in the promotion of values and conundrums held by people of flesh and bone.

Reason is to have a vital function, Unamuno argues. Since our greatest, most vital problem has to do with the destiny of human consciousness (against the nihilistic view that our lives, qua mortal, have no inherent significance), the philosophy of "reason" is actually an enemy of life. That might be what is most tragic in *Tragic Sense of Life*: reason, the faculty that was crafted by humans to deal with their mortal state, now fights against our vital longings, even converting God into a deistic ideal instead of the Living God—the Catholic God, the God that answers our longings about immortality. For Unamuno, the only way human beings are immortal is if God exists. There is no reason to care whether God exists if it does not pertain to our vital longing for immortality. Rationalism (versus scholasticism, which continued in Spain well into the twentieth century) denies this longing, even to the point of declaring itself an enemy of vitalism:

> there is also an anti-theological advocacy, and an *odium anti-theologicum*. Many, very many, men of science, the majority of those who call themselves rationalists, are afflicted by it. The

rationalist acts rationally . . . so long as he confines himself to
denying that reason satisfies our vital hunger for immortality.[29]

This rationalism culminates in two possible ways: either a Spinozist monism
where God is simply the comprehensive ideal of all things or a Nietzschean
atheism. For Unamuno, Nietzsche's declaration that "God is dead" signi-
fies that, reduced to the ultimate rational ordering of the universe—*Deus
sive natura*—there is no reason to continue with the God project. The God
project had a vital goal: immortality. Upon reducing God to simply issues of
the origin of the universe, for example, science easily replaces religion, leaving religion as a remnant of prescientific thinking and superstition. With
religion removed from the modern European equation, there is no place
for the vital longing for immortality. Hence the despair of Europe in the
twentieth century. Although Unamuno died in 1936, in the opening months
of the Spanish Civil War (which many historians claim technically set up
the Second World War), the atrocities of twentieth-century Europe can be
traced back to the state of affairs Unamuno described in 1912. With God
out of the equation, what would vouchsafe the value of the human person?

Hence Unamuno's use of the term "faith" as the efforts against this
rationalization and consequent death of God. It is of vital importance to
believe in God, even if one could not square that belief with rationalism.
Thus, Unamuno is taught as a fideist. Yet this reading (which I myself have
taught, but will no longer) removes Unamuno's argument from his historical context. Instead, *Tragic Sense of Life* shares Hook's hope in his address:
philosophy has to be able to address and think through the choices we
make—intellectual or moral.

In the penultimate chapter of *Tragic Sense of Life*, "The Practical Problem," Unamuno writes the following about his worry about Spanish identity
in the face of European "reason":

> And since we Spaniards are Catholic—whether we know it or
> not, and whether we like it or not—and although some of us
> may claim to be rationalists or atheists, perhaps the greatest
> service we can render to the cause of culture, and of what is of
> more value than culture, religiousness—if indeed they are not
> the same thing—is in endeavoring to formulate clearly to our-
> selves this subconscious, social, or popular Catholicism of ours.
> And that is what I have attempted to do in this work.
>
> What I call the tragic sense of life in men and peoples is
> at any rate our tragic sense of life, that of Spaniards and the
> Spanish people, as it is reflected in my consciousness, which is

29. Unamuno, *Tragic Sense of Life*, 95.

a Spanish consciousness, made in Spain. And this tragic sense
of life is essentially the Catholic sense of it, for Catholicism, and
above all popular Catholicism, is tragic.[30]

In light of increased Europeanization, insistence of the Spanish Catholic
way of life will be tragic. The question will be whether it can become also
comical, a parody of European "reason."

Unamuno concludes *Tragic Sense of Life* with a discussion of Don
Quixote as tragic figure and as parody of European "reason." Unamuno
realizes that his own anguish is unnecessary; he despairs because he had
adopted the European standard of "reason," which critiqued his own self-
loved Spanish life. We see a glimpse of this in the following passage:

> there is another, more tragic Inquisition, and that is the Inqui-
> sition which the modern man, the man of culture, the Euro-
> pean—and such am I, whether I will or not—carries within
> him. There is a more terrible ridicule, and that is the ridicule
> with which a man contemplates his own self. It is my reason that
> laughs at my faith and despises it.
>
> And it is here that I must betake me to my Lord Don
> Quixote in order that I may learn [from] him how to confront
> ridicule and overcome it, and a ridicule which perhaps—who
> knows?—he never knew.
>
> Yes, yes—how shall my reason not smile at these dilet-
> tantesque, would-be mystical, pseudo-philosophical interpre-
> tations, in which there is anything rather than patient study
> and—shall I say scientific?—objectivity and method?[31]

To take on the tragic sense of life, one must be able to confront ridicule,
embrace what is being mocked by others, and "make a fool of oneself," just
as Don Quixote did as the errant Spanish scholastic knight confronting the
rise of European rationalism. The classical Don Quixote was willing to be
ridiculous in the eyes of European modernity. This is what makes him a
hero. This is what makes him immortal. Although everyone mocked Don
Quixote, Alonzo Quijano's actions were actually mocking them. Hence,
Don Quixote is both tragic and comic: tragicomic.

As we will see in the next section, the Black experience is Quixotic
insofar as it is tragic but also tragicomic. A culture that is mocked becomes
a site for laughter and insight. Without dealing with the tragic, philosophy
runs the risk of becoming aloof and, even worse, oppressive and anti-
vital. If philosophy, however, comes from the tragic and the vital, it can

---

30. Unamuno, *Tragic Sense of Life*, 295.

31. Unamuno, *Tragic Sense of Life*, 302.

be empowering and liberatory. As I will argue in chapter 7, Baldwin and Levinas show us that the lack of tragedy in the white experience, white enjoyment (*jouissance*), perpetuates violence. Meanwhile, Black tragedy will produce freedom for all Americans, including whites trapped in their own enjoyment.

PROPHETIC PRAGMATISM, TRAGEDY, AND THE TRAGICOMIC

Philosophy and Tragedy in The American Evasion of Philosophy

Before moving on to the discussion of West's essays in *Keeping Faith*, I explore in this section West's discussion of tragedy in the final chapter of his *The American Evasion of Philosophy* (1989). In this book, West highlights the Emersonian foundation of American thought, offering a genealogy from Emerson to his own thought. A key section of the final chapter is titled "Tragedy, Tradition, and Political Praxis." Although I am not interested in the political dimension of West's thought in this essay, I do want to highlight West's view of tragedy discussed here since it predates the discussion of tragedy in *Keeping Faith*.

West defines prophetic pragmatism in this section as a philosophy that "affirms the Niebuhrian strenuous mood, never giving up on new possibilities for human agency—both individual and collective—in the present, yet situating them in light of DuBois' social structural analyses that focus on working-class, black, and female insurgency."[32] This is a corrective to Richard Rorty's politically inert self-creationist neopragmatism that, although perhaps sufficient for white "bourgeois postmodernists" (Rorty's term), is unfortunately insufficient for the Black freedom struggle.[33]

To do this, West begins by distinguishing between Greek tragedy and modern American tragedy. Greek tragedy, West writes, is grounded in "a society that shares a collective experience of common metaphysical and social meanings."[34] In a somewhat hegemonic society, the plot of Greek

32. West, *The American Evasion of Philosophy*, 228.

33. West outlines his critique of Rorty's (white) bourgeois neopragmatism in chapter 5 of *The American Evasion of Philosophy*, drawing from previous critiques of Rorty found in his review of Rorty's *Philosophy and the Mirror of Nature*, published in the *Union Seminary Quarterly Review*, and his afterword, "The Politics of American Neo-Pragmatism," published in *Post-Analytic Philosophy*.

34. West, *The American Evasion of Philosophy*, 227.

tragedy was always about the ways that the gods amuse themselves at the expense of human endeavoring. This is not the sense of tragedy that defines our present-day American context. Instead, as West writes, the modern (American) sense of tragedy is situated in a context where "ordinary individuals struggle against meaninglessness and nothingness" in "a fragmented society with collapsing metaphysical meanings."[35] Additionally, in modern tragedy (whether or not it is American), there is more of a focus on the actions of individuals. We see this, for example, in Shakespearean tragedy, where the tragic flaw of a character (be it Hamlet's brooding or Macbeth's self-assurance) creates the situation and their downfall.

In the modern American setting, tragedy centers on "the irreducible predicament of unique individuals who undergo dread, despair, disillusionment, disease, and death *and* the institutional forms of oppression that dehumanize people."[36] In West's case, racism, with its overt and covert implications on the situations, efforts, and values of Americans, is one of several tragic elements that we must face and somehow deal with as part of our thinking. It is no longer divine (as it was with the Greeks), but evil—the evil produced by choices based on and grounded in deliberate *human* systems of oppression.

Prophetic pragmatism's first response to this tragic evil is to realize that oppression is "neither inevitable nor necessary but rather the results of human agency."[37] The story of American racism (along with other forms of oppression) is the consequence of contingency, a combination of historical parameters and individual and collective choices. It did not have to be this way.[38] As a result, Black people have had to form themselves out of a tragic situation.[39] The responses of Black people did not seek to deny the reality or remove the existence of this evil; rather, the Black tradition was forged in response to it, facing the issue head-on in the hope of creating lives of meaning. These "strivings," as West would call them in homage to W. E. B. DuBois,[40] serve as the set of practices that prophetic pragmatism seeks to make intelligible.[41]

35. West, *The American Evasion of Philosophy*, 227.
36. West, *The American Evasion of Philosophy*, 228.
37. West, *The American Evasion of Philosophy*, 228.
38. Hence West's genealogy of racism in light of the development of the United States as outlined in chs. 1 and 2 of *Prophesy Deliverance!*
39. This is explained in the second half of West's 1977 article, "Philosophy and the Afro-American Experience," which would become ch. 3 of *Prophesy Deliverance!*
40. Cf. West, "Black Strivings in a Twilight Civilization" in West and Gates, *The Future of the Race*.
41. Cf. Stone, "Making Religious Practices Intelligible," 137–53. Also cf. Stone, "Making Religious Practices Intelligible in the Public Sphere."

But this tragic sense of philosophizing that governs West's prophetic pragmatism from an African American perspective is not merely for Black people. It serves as a framework for all who think from a modern American tragic situation in the hope of thinking through evil and staying committed to the struggle for self-determination, self-creation, and social progress. He writes,

> Human struggle sits at the center of prophetic pragmatism, a struggle guided by a democratic and libertarian vision, sustained by moral courage and existential integrity, and tempered by the recognition of human finitude and frailty. It calls for utopian energies and tragic actions, energies and actions that yield permanent and perennial revolutionary, rebellious, and reformist strategies that oppose the status quos of our day. These strategies are never to become ends-in-themselves, but rather to remain means through which are channeled moral outrage and human desperation in the face of prevailing forms of evil in human societies and in human lives. Such outrage must never cease, and such desperation will never disappear, yet without revolutionary, rebellious, and reformist strategies, credible and effective opposition wanes.[42]

Prophetic pragmatism, to borrow from one of my favorite hymns, is a way to "let the lower lights be burning" in the hope of guiding sailors on the stormy seas safely home. It perpetually re-energizes resistance to oppression by critically engaging with the reality of the evil with which we find ourselves. Philosophy as a whole, West argues, should be this quest. Prophetic pragmatism is a philosophy that does not "ignore . . . the ugly facts and unpleasant realities of life and history. Rather, it highlights these facts and realities."[43] It "condemns oppression anywhere and everywhere."[44] Firmly rooted in the American tradition of struggle and self-reliance described by Emerson, prophetic pragmatism avoids ideological illusions about what is happening in our world and aids the struggle of oppressed groups by highlighting the wisdom found in such groups' efforts to directly respond to tragic situations. It grants the tragic reality of "what is" while striving "to change *what is* into a better *what can be*."[45]

---

42. West, *The American Evasion of Philosophy*, 229.
43. West, *The American Evasion of Philosophy*, 230.
44. West, *The American Evasion of Philosophy*, 235.
45. West, *The American Evasion of Philosophy*, 230; emphasis added.

Reading Royce as Philosopher of the Tragic

In the preface to *Keeping Faith*, West describes prophetic criticism (pragmatism) as

> the existential imperative to institutionalize critiques of illegitimate authority and arbitrary uses of power; a bestowal of dignity, grandeur and tragedy on the ordinary lives of people; and an experimental form of life that highlights curiosity, wonder, contingency, adventure, danger and, most importantly, improvisation. These elements constitute a democratic mode of being in the world inseparable from democratic ways of life and ways of struggle.[46]

West's motives for exploring prophetic criticism is couched here in terms of the double consciousness of African Americans, who are the mixture of New World African sensibilities and European Enlightenment culture. For the sake of this chapter, I will not explore the philosophy of race laid out by West in this book, although it is an important context for his analysis.

West begins "Pragmatism and the Sense of the Tragic" by highlighting three key American figures and their corresponding key American tenants: Thomas Jefferson, whose "notions of the irreducibility of individuality within participatory communities attempt to sidestep rapacious individualism and authoritarian communitarianisms"; Ralph Waldo Emerson, whose "formulations of heroic action of ordinary folk in a world of radical contingency try to jettison static dogmatisms and impersonal determinisms"; and Abraham Lincoln, whose "profound wrestling with a deep sense of evil that fuels struggle for justice endeavors to hold at bay facile optimisms and paralyzing pessimisms."[47] West laments that "not one American *philosophical* thinker has put forward a conception of the meaning and significance of democracy in light of these foundations laid by Jefferson, Emerson, and Lincoln."[48] Of course, West seeks in this essay to be or become that American philosophical thinker.

After highlighting the ways that Royce and Dewey fulfill the three "philosophical slogans" of pragmatism (voluntarism, fallibilism, and experimentalism—which I will address in chapter 5), West offers a reading of Royce's account of the Absolute as a key example of a philosopher truly taking up tragedy and evil. Quoting from Royce's 1912 *Sources of Religious Insight*, West zeroes in on a key element of the Absolute as it pertains to

46. West, *Keeping Faith*, xi.

47. West, *Keeping Faith*, 107–08.

48. West, *Keeping Faith*, 108.

choices and actions: "every deed once done is *ipso facto* irrevocable. That is, at any moment you perform a given deed or you do not. If you perform it, it is done and cannot be undone."[49] Here we see a key theme already developed by Hook in different terms: to deal with the tragic is to recognize that choices have true consequences and costs. One cannot undo what has been chosen; one can simply mitigate the costs and consequences.

West then focuses on a passage from Royce's *The Spirit of Modern Philosophy*, where Royce defends the Absolute against "the capricious irrationality of the world" and "the blind irrationality of fortune."[50] It would truly be tragic if our choices did not matter at all (as Hook said about not being able to die), or if the consequences were not connected to our choices. For Royce, the worry that the world might be arbitrary or random is resolved by an appeal to idealism. From the finite point of view, "there is no remotely discoverable justification for this caprice"; yet, Royce says (and West quotes) we must "dare to hope for an answer . . . What in time is hopelessly lost, is attained for him in his eternity."[51] Here we see a connection to Unamuno's vital longing for immortality, not to become something other than we are (mortal), but to gain the fulfilment of our conscious choices in some nonarbitrary way.

West abruptly ends the essay here, commenting that indeed Royce has taken up the issue of the tragic; thus, pragmatism has the ability to take up the tragic (which in turn allows West's prophetic pragmatism to take up the tragicomic).

I would be remiss if I did not say more about Royce's notion of evil. In West's essay on Royce, West writes that he will only focus on Royce's notion of irrevocable deeds as an expression of the Absolute while skipping Royce's famous essays on evil. My best conjecture about why West did this is that West wished to limit the role of idealism, for which West criticizes Royce. Yet, for an essay *on* Royce, especially about Royce being one of the few American thinkers to take Lincoln's emphasis on evil seriously, it is strange not to give Royce's answer to the problem of evil. For the sake of completeness (and given its connection to my reading of Unamuno), I wish to summarize Royce's "The Problem of Job"—which West considers one of Royce's "rich reflections on evil" but which he does "not plunge into."[52]

Written in 1897 to think through and respond to "the genuine experience of suffering humanity" that Royce takes the Book of Job to be,[53] Royce

49. West, *Keeping Faith*, 114, citing Royce, *Sources of Religious Insight*, 153.
50. West, *Keeping Faith*, 115.
51. West, *Keeping Faith*, 117.
52. West, *Keeping Faith*, 114.
53. Royce, "The Problem of Job," 85.

offers a defense of idealism as a nonabstract solution to the problem of evil. Of course, the problem of evil is a perennial philosophical question. Royce begins by presenting and refuting the standard responses to the problem of evil. Royce rejects responses that deny that there is such a thing as "evil." He thinks this results from an unwillingness to see the world as teleological. For something to be evil, it would have to be something that hinders or frustrates what was supposed to happen. Royce also rejects responses that believe that God allows evil in order to accomplish some greater good. This treats evil as merely transitory or as some step in an evolutionary process. Royce argues instead that one must treat evil as "a logical necessity."[54] There *must* be evil. Why?

The third response that Royce rejects is the free-will defense. Royce correctly notes that the argument from Job's friends that Job must have done something wrong in order to deserve his suffering is precisely what is being refuted in the Scripture. Evil is not a consequence of our actions, nor is it some karmic debt from a previous life's choices. Job correctly claims his righteousness; he has not done anything wrong, so his suffering is not the result of free will.

Royce's response to the problem of evil, and to the Book of Job, offers an idealist solution not only to the problem of evil but the very problem of the relationship between human beings and God. He writes:

> The answer to Job is: God is not in ultimate essence another being than yourself. He is the Absolute Being. You truly are one with God, part of his life. He is the very soul of your soul . . . When you suffer, *your sufferings are God's sufferings*, not his external work, not his external penalty, not the fruit of his neglect, but identically his own personal woe. In you God himself suffers.[55]

The problem of evil is not that God "causes" or "allows" us (as if we are distinct from God in any ontological sense) to experience evil; it is the simple fact that God suffers, and *our* suffering is simply that God suffers. The difference between God and the one facing misfortune is one of parts and the whole. God understands "why bad things happen to good people," because God sees the entire picture (hence God's questions to Job in response to Job's accusations: "Where were you when I created the universe?" (Job 38:4)). Job, as any suffering human being, knows only their finite part of the whole; the suffering human does not have a large enough frame of reference. Royce generalizes this claim, concluding that "[i]t is logically impossible that a complete knower of truth should fail to know, to experience, to have present

54. Royce, "The Problem of Job," 91.
55. Royce, "The Problem of Job," 95.

to his insight, the fact of actually existing evil."[56] Somehow, evil is necessary, not for the sake of the good, but for the sake of perfection: "The existence of evil, then, is not only consistent with the perfection of the universe, but is necessary for the very existence of that perfection."[57] Somehow, evil makes the world "complete."

One can see why West did not explore this essay. Since West resists idealism, he is not interested in idealist solutions to the problem of evil. Following Emerson, West will want creative solutions—dare we say, Promethean solutions—to our suffering. Hence, Royce is lauded by West for taking on the problem of evil in the spirit of Lincoln, but West is proposing a different response than Royce.

Prophetic Pragmatism and the Tragicomic

The theme of the tragic (and the tragicomic) runs throughout the entirety of West's writings. Although West more frequently mentions Anton Chekhov instead of Miguel de Unamuno, the centrality of tragedy is a necessary condition for pragmatism's quest for ameliorative hope, which serves as a critical lens through which to interpret and critique Pollyanna-ish philosophies of hope.

In his introduction to *The Cornel West Reader*, West describes himself as "a Chekhovian Christian with deep democratic commitments. By this I mean that I am obsessed with confronting the pervasive evil of unjustified suffering and unnecessary social misery in our world."[58] Unlike Royce, West finds suffering and social misery (especially the suffering and misery of Black people in America) to be *unnecessary* and *unjustified*. Like Royce, this evil is real and must be dealt with. Like Unamuno, West agrees that "[t]o be human is to suffer, shudder and struggle courageously in the face of inevitable death" and that we are to "focus on particular, singular, flesh-and-blood persons grappling with dire issues of death, dread, despair, disease and disappointment."[59] West's view of evil and the tragic sense of life is materially grounded in the existential plight of Black people who seek to have lives of meaning and purpose in a world bent on denying Blacks their humanity. Yet, there is no room for pessimism in West's philosophy. Although Black people constitute "the night side of American democracy," a phrase he frequently uses, "I highlight the forms of self-making and self-creating of

56. Royce, "The Problem of Job," 103.
57. Royce, "The Problem of Job," 104.
58. West, *The Cornel West Reader*, xv.
59. West, *The Cornel West Reader*, xvi–xvii.

those whose suffering is often rendered invisible."[60] Through West's corpus, we find examinations of Black self-creation, especially in terms of Black theology and Black music.

This self-creation in light of misery is what West means by the word "tragicomic." Black people are tragicomic insofar as they have crafted an identity and destiny in light of the tragic sense of being Black in racist America. Like Chekhov and other Russian thinkers that inspire West, Black people "had to explore the fundamental issues of what it means to be human: to wrestle with the problem of evil, to live an intense life in the face of death, to grapple with democratic possibilities and with social justice."[61] Black people have found a way to hold on to something like the American Dream, not as *jouissance* or optimism, but as a goal to create. One must overcome tragedy and produce beauty, justice, and human dignity.

To do this, one must be mindful of the tragic and the comic as interpretive lenses. As West writes, "I understand [the] tragic to refer to the freedom that humans have to explore the possibility of even great freedom, but against constraints of which they are unaware. The comic is a way of acknowledging those limitations and the incongruity between those high aspirations and where one actually ends up."[62] Constrained by the tragic, the comic pushes us heroically to greater situations, fully aware that the situation and sometimes we ourselves hinder the proposed progress. West presents Chekhov as the highest exemplar of this tension between the tragic and the comic, although one can find it just as readily in the Black experience.

In *Democracy Matters*, West highlights tragicomic hope as one of the three moral pillars of democracy alongside Socratic questioning and prophetic witness. He says the following about tragicomic hope:

> In the face of cynical and disillusioned acquiescence to the status quo, we must draw on the tragicomic. Tragicomic hope is a profound attitude toward life reflected in the world of artistic geniuses as diverse as Lucian in the Roman empire, Cervantes in the Spanish empire, and Chekhov in the Russian empire. Within the American empire it has been most powerfully expressed in the black invention of the blues in the face of white supremacist powers.[63]

60. West, *The Cornel West Reader*, xviii.
61. West, *The Cornel West Reader*, 555.
62. West, *The Cornel West Reader*, 557.
63. West, *Democracy Matters*, 19.

Notice that tragicomic hope is not idealism but radical creativity, an "attitude towards life" based on suffering while nonetheless elevating the human spirit.[64]

West's work seeks to teach philosophy how to sing the blues. As I have mentioned in my chapter on the blues in *Introducing Prophetic Pragmatism*, the blues offer us a way to confront tragedy in a creative way that fully expresses the human reality of overcoming what brings us down. The blues are *melancholic*—literally, "black," melanin, visceral. As West sings in "Blues Stomp," the blues are "visceral, cerebral / connect that gut to the soul, that mind to the heart."[65]

Prophetic pragmatism, insofar as it fully embraces the tragic sense of life, is indeed pragmatism at its best. It is a thinking that inspires radical hope in the face of what attempts to frustrate our plans and dreams. It is, as Hook reminds us, a creative intelligence that frees us from the evils we face without dismissing those evils in the name of other goods. Instead, it forces a conflict of values and rights that opens up for us choices, consequences, and ideas. As such, it is "dangerous—and potentially subversive—because it can never be extinguished . . . it is inexorably resilient and inescapably seductive—even contagious."[66]

64. See West, *Democracy Matters*, 19.
65. West, "Blues Stomp," track 17 in *Street Knowledge*.
66. West, *Democracy Matters*, 217.

3

A Cacophony of Cries:
All Cries Are Not Created Equal

Philip R. Kuehnert

> Abel's blood for vengeance
>
> Pleaded to the skies,
>
> But the blood of Jesus
>
> For our pardon cries.[1]

NOT FAIR!

THE DEBACLE IN THE garden of Eden, which imagination strains to conjure up a worse situation than, is followed by a fratricide that initiates the first silent cry. That primordial silent cry, and all past and future cascading echoes, is given voice through the ages ultimately in Jesus' cry of dereliction from the cross. That same Jesus punctuated his teachings with the cry: "He who has ears, let him hear" (Matt 11:15). Beloved communities strain to hear.

---

1. From the hymn "Glory Be to Jesus," in *Lutheran Book of Worship*, no. 95.

As a rainbow baby,[2] I was welcomed and celebrated with cries of joy, not only by my parents and three older siblings, but by many friends and relatives who three years earlier had joined their cries with the cry of my parents at the stillbirth of my sister, Paula Hope. I was well into my fifth decade when I discovered that my mother had saved those cries of celebration for me. She had carefully saved them in an old card box, saving the notes, letters, and congratulatory cards that my parents received from around the country, including several from my father's relatives in Germany. All that did not inoculate me from echoing, for decades, not Abel's cry, but Cain's silent cry.

Occasionally, I am stunned out of my isolation by the cry of others. The first time I saw the movie *Amadeus*, the opening scene of a young priest's visit to ancient Salieri after a failed suicide shocked me. As Salieri ranted about the unfairness of God in granting the profane Mozart extraordinary gifts while denying his desire, I was unexpectedly stunned—not understanding what was going on. It was only on subsequent viewings (and there have been many) that I began to realize that Salieri's cry was a cry that had haunted me for decades. Similarly, my cry "not fair" was about my mediocre musical ability. My cry "not fair" was amplified by growing up in the shadow of two older and gifted brothers. Identifying my cry of "not fair" with Cain's and Salieri's murderous impulses has surfaced in a vague memory in which, at about the age of twelve, I came up behind my older brother who was sitting in a Radio Flyer wagon and broke a broom handle over his head.

In relation to the outsized attention on the wounds inflicted by God on Jesus, little attention has been paid to the wound that God inflicted on Cain. The former is an emphatic reminder that undeserved wounds can be redemptive. The latter and its silent cry is the first expression of a wounded world. For decades, I looked for affirmation of my silent cry.

Surprisingly, I found affirmation in James Melvin Washington's *Conversations with God: Two Centuries of Prayers by African Americans.* Washington concludes the anthology with his own prayer, entitled "Afterword: A Scholar's Benediction." An excerpt:

> Malfeasance, malice, and even murder have become scandalous dog-ears in the macabre texts of the newest versions of barbarity that bedevil the twentieth century . . . Your archives reveal past prayers that engaged the creeping issues of theodicy that threaten to sour our covenant with Thee. Only you know how

2. For years, I had called myself a celebration baby. Several years ago, I discovered that rainbow baby is now popularly used to describe the a baby born following the death of an infant.

many of your black children are angry with you. Like Cain, it is easier to kill Abel than to admit anger with our Divine Parent. Some of us scream, "Why do you favor Abel, especially when Abel has more than he needs?" Your silence pains us. Our souls demand justice.[3]

The stories of Cain, Abel, and Jesus were preserved and retold by beloved communities. Has there ever been a murderer who has not tasted the bile of Cain? Has there even been an Abel whose blood has not cried out for vengeance? Has there ever been a victim of chronic abuse or systemic racism that has not screamed or at least thought, "Why is God silent? Why has God abandoned me?" Has there ever been a sibling that has not cried out at the injustice of why parents chose to "bless" another, or why one has to live in the shadow of another sibling's greatness/talent/good looks? The *ideal* of the Beloved Community promises at least a hearing, if not a hearing with God's ears.[4] The reality is that too often communities, families, and societies not only close their collective ears but, when the cries of Abel and Cain appear in their midst, they are unable to provide a hearing, much less a place. The unending appeal of beloved community is in part due to the way it has traditionally provided a place for the cries to be expressed and, more importantly, a hearing and, finally, an affirmation. The stories of and the continuing prophetic message of the Scriptures of the Abrahamic traditions is a continual reminder that the community is in some sense the ears of God. Just as important is the constant resource of the literature to give voice to the cry in the stories, poetry, psalms, laments, and wisdom that constitute a major part of them. The Scriptures of Christianity, Islam, and Judaism preserve the story of Cain and Abel, but not without comment.

It seems that all traditions will not accept the arbitrary nature of God's gifting and withholding gifts without struggle and argument. The basic assumption is that life is fair. Or is it? Scriptures reflect the challenge of that struggle. The story of Cain and Abel is the story of Cain, unsuccessful, in spite of God's warning, to accept that life is not fair. Examples abound: Moses resisting God's call and then displaying attitude throughout most of his career; Jacob's wrestling with God; the agonizing arguments of Job and his friends; the catastrophic implosion of both the Northern and Southern kingdoms and the desperate attempt of the prophetic traditions to make sense of it; Jesus refusing to affirm the theodicy of first-century Judaism in

---

3. Washington, *Conversations*, 284.

4. Willie Young provides a deeply analytical assessment of the importance of listening: "As God's ears, religious regimes of listening create social, corporate forms of embodiment that open transformative possibilities of sensibility" (Young, *Listening, Religion, and Democracy in Contemporary Boston*, 157).

John 9; Paul's struggle in Romans 9–11 with God's chosen people rejecting Jesus as Messiah; and, finally, the apocalyptic struggle of good vs. evil in the Book of Revelation.

Scripture itself adds to the problem. Scripture is the source of the struggle. On the one hand, God is—in the words of pouting Jonah—"a God gracious and compassionate, long-suffering and ever constant, and always willing to repent of disaster" (Jonah 4:2–3). The Johannine texts emphasize the God who is love incarnate, offers life, and life in abundance and life eternal. On the other hand, Scripture depicts a God who loses patience and a God who—based on commitment or lack of commitment—will either reward with long life, wealth, and many children or immediate death by fire, plague, or earthquake.

The Beloved Community is the crucible in which living human documents are thrown into the scriptural traditions in an ongoing attempt to find distinctive echoes in the cacophony of cries. It is the cacophony in which the silent cries are given as much attention as the cries which scream. The vibrancy of the beloved communities depend on their ability to provide a place where the gifted, the mediocre, and the not-abled are equally celebrated. Where they not only have a place, but their cries are heard, valued, and responded to—their unique cries adding to the richness of life for all.

THE BELOVED COMMUNITY AND THE CACOPHONY: "I HAVE HEARD THEIR CRY ON ACCOUNT OF THEIR TASKMASTERS" (EXOD 3:7)

The previous section developed the primordial cry of "not fair." What follows seeks to explore the complexity of the human cry and how the beloved communities provide the place and the sounding board for the cry. As the ears of God, beloved communities cannot but respond to the cries—although its effectiveness depends on how well it prepares itself to listen.

In the fall of 1976, our young family moved from the Lower Ninth Ward of New Orleans to the Buckhead area of Atlanta. Shortly after we moved, parishioners invited my wife and me to attend a concert by the Atlanta Symphony Orchestra in Symphony Hall of the Memorial Arts Center. It was the first time I attended a major symphony orchestra. Musicians were gathering on the stage. What struck me was the growing cacophony as more and more instruments added their voices. The piercing shriek of the piccolo was tamed by the double basses and in between were the thrilling arpeggios of trumpets and clarinets and the incessant sawing of the strings. Suddenly, there was quiet as a strange pantomime/drama unfolded before me. I learned later this is a ritual for orchestras, where a man or woman, the concert master or mistress, traditionally the first violinist, walks on stage, motions to the oboe, who plays an A, and then, suddenly, all instruments in their various ranges tune to the A. The cacophony is gone. The conductor walks on stage, receives applause, shakes the concert master/mistress hand, steps on the podium, and the concert begins.

Without stretching the metaphor too far, this image of the cacophony in the concert hall moving to the beauty and magnificence of a concert carries with it a powerful promise. If beloved communities are *tuned* to the cries of the world, there will be a surge of cries from history—amplified in the present crises of a pandemic, the rise in domestic violence, and political chaos—to a deafening cacophony. And then, as the community gathers, disparate parts, each with his or her own unique cry, finds a place and is heard.[5] The cacophony of cries rising up from a wounded world demands a response.

It is at this point that the resources of beloved communities, beginning with their facility to identify and interpret cries, heed and tend to, and if necessary echo and blend, the cries in a redemptive way. Scripture and the extended history of beloved communities are filled with stories of redemption. Beloved communities ought to be well aware of their limitations. They seek to be wise in the way they honor the cries of the world and the cries of their members without being held hostage to them. Beloved communities hear and discern the cacophony of cries arising from a wounded world.

This is where the traditions of the community, in Scripture and ritual, prove their worth. The wounds that produce the cries are analyzed, sometimes critically from theological or philosophical bases. The collective wisdom of the community prevents either looking away or not hearing. Whatever work is done it is always with the intent of honoring the wounds and providing a place for the resulting cries with the understanding/belief that the cries provide the glue that holds the community together.

Taxonomy is the science of classification, useful when distinguishing subsets of a general category. David F. Ford, in his *Christian Wisdom: Desiring God and Learning in Love*, provides what I consider a helpful taxonomy of cries. The apsis of cries is the human cry of dereliction and the cry of "He is risen." All cries, including the cry of silence, fall somewhere between those two. The nonverbal cry—the primal scream—of the human gives expression to the extremes of human experience from agony to ecstasy. I believe that Ford, in identifying these moods, provides a rich resource for beloved communities. A primary role of the community is to provide discernment in

5. The children's song, "A Place in the Choir," by Bill Staines, comes to mind.

identifying cries in the cacophony rising up from the wounded world, but also in providing an attentive and responsive ear to the cries that arise from within the community itself.

David Ford's moods of cries provides beloved communities with the hermeneutical skill to discern and respond. Ford succinctly expresses his thesis:

> The more I have searched for Christian wisdom, the more I have been struck by its core connection with cries: the cries for wisdom and the cries by the personified biblical wisdom, cries within and outside of scripture that arise from the intensities of life—in joy, suffering, recognition, wonder, bewilderment, gratitude, expectation or acclamation; and cries of people for what they most desire—love, justice, truth, goodness, compassion, children, health, food and drink, education, security and so on. Christian wisdom is discerned within earshot of such cries, and is above all alert to the cries of Jesus.[6]

While David Ford identifies five moods of cries, two moods—the indicative and the imperative—are strident in their urgency. The indicative sounds the alarm. The original cry (silent) of Cain, "not fair," has been echoed through the centuries. The interrogative cries, "Why?"; "Who is responsible?"; "What does this mean?" are reflexive for the human. The two cries together demand a beloved community to be ready and able to provide usable theodicies, or failing that, to provide at least a response. So how can a loving, all-powerful, and all-knowing God cause/allow suffering/injustice/genocides? Those who have stood in defense of God have gone to extremes to deny reality and, unfortunately, to actively mute cries. I pluralize theodicy—theod*ies*—because there is no theodicy that fits all or that adequately responds to the cries that constitute the cacophony.

Two relatively recent books call out false theodicies so often offered unthinkingly to those who are in crisis, those victims of trauma who have lost their voice, and those who are in the shock of having their lives instantly changed. In their autobiographical stories, Kate Bowler's *Everything Happens for a Reason: And Other Lies I've Loved*, and Jacqueline A. Bussie's *Outlaw Christian: Finding Authentic Faith by Breaking the Rules*, relate how they have had to overcome the often unthinking platitudes that are intended to explain the unexplainable and defend the indefensible. Each of them have come out on the other side with their faith intact but profoundly changed because of the trajectories of their lives. Fred Niedner, in his extensive work

---

6. Ford, *Christian Wisdom*, 4.

on the wilderness traditions in Scripture suggests that, in spite of our "addiction to theodicy," there may be no usable theodicy.[7]

The men who have come to be known as the disciples/apostles/saints matured in the context of cries: their own cries, the cries of the sick and the cries of those who cared for the sick, the cries of those who challenged Jesus, and finally the cries of Jesus himself. All of this finds affirmation in David's Ford's *Christian Wisdom*. The underlying *cantus firmus* of Ford's book, honoring Christian/biblical wisdom, becomes the centrality of cries. Ford establishes the basis for cry and response not only being the basis for a beloved community but also necessary for the healing of a wounded world. On one extreme, we have Jesus on the cross crying out with what has become known as the seven last words from the cross, to the wounded and resurrected Christ inviting discipleship to share a beachside breakfast which he has prepared for them.

Ford offers a profound challenge to the community in its role of discerning cries. He offers two tools. The first is exploring faith from the perspective of five moods rooted in cries. In the following, Ford helps us understand what he means by each of the moods.

> The indicative that affirms or denies, the imperative of command and obedience; the interrogative that questions, probes, suspects and tests; the subjunctive exploring the possibilities of what may or might be, alert to surprises; and the optative of desire . . . The theological wisdom of faith is grounded in being affirmed, being commanded, being questioned and searched [interrogative], being surprised and open to new possibilities and being desired and loved.[8]

Exploring the faith from the perspective of the moods might take this form.

Indicative

"The pattern of affirmation rooted in being affirmed by God is at the core of the confession of Christian faith. . . . narrative is the main form of the indicative in historical mode."[9] This mood unleashes the power to bless, to name, to curse, to declare, to judge. In sacramental traditions, great power is given to the words, "I baptize you, [name] in the name of the . . ." and in the

---

7. Niedner, "Lament and Sustenance," 12.

8. Ford, *Christian Wisdom*, 5.

9. Ford, *Christian Wisdom*, 46; emphasis in original.

words, "this is the body of . . . the blood of Christ."[10] The cry of "Repent, the Kingdom of heaven is at hand" initiated a new reality still celebrated today (Matt 4:7). Jesus' cry at the beginning of his ministry "today this Scripture has been fulfilled in your ears" unleased opposition that would finally result in his crucifixion (Luke 4:21).

Imperative

The cries of "Run!" and "Fire!" indicate immediate danger. On the level of faith, the imperative provides the sinews that hold the community of faith together. From "Repent!" to "so this" raises to a level of consciousness how much of the life of beloved community is based on the assumption of obedience.[11] The imperatives, "Go!"; "Teach!"; "Be baptized!"; "Listen to Him!"; etc. These imperatives invite an obedience which provides structure to beloved community.

Interrogative

Questioning and being questioned is the lifeblood of creativity in the Beloved Community. The beloved community that developed around Jesus was structured on the incessant questioning of Jesus and by Jesus. Answers—good, false, ambiguous, correct—give structure to what is important and leaves discarded that which is not. The very nature of the Beloved Community is based on having answers to certain questions, initiating and continuing discussions in response to other questions, and evading giving answers to other questions. The perennial cries demanding that God's actions be defended or explained are among the most important for a community that intends to be faithful and responsive.

Subjunctive

The marriage of the interrogative with the subjective provides an incubator for the creativity that mimics God's creativity in art, music, and literature. The delight of the subjunctive is that surprising future unfolds in the

10. Lutheran Church Missouri Synod, *Lutheran Service Book*, 268, 151.

11. Young, *Listening, Religion, and Democracy in Contemporary Boston*, 133. Young brings the obvious to the forefront in his ethnographic study of the different levels of listening—to the cries?—of the communities and how dependent on obedience is the effective response. See especially chapter 5, entitled "Defiant Obedience" (133–50).

nebulous dimension of hope. Scripture and the history of the traditions of faith communities testify to the mystery of how the possible became reality. Immersion in the subjunctive allows the Beloved Community to always be open to the surprises that constitute life. Here the Beloved Community imagines possibilities, debates options, and makes decisions.

Optative

In the Greek, the optative mood expresses desire, wishes, with conditional statements: "If only . . ."; "May it be . . ." The Beloved Community reflects in its purpose specific wishes of what it can be to those who are part of the community and for those outside of its walls. In Scripture, the desire is for place and for people. The "promised land," while never fully realized, continues to be important for the Jewish people in differing iterations from cries pertaining to Jerusalem in the annual Passover to the Zionist movement.

The second tool Ford offers the community in its role of discerning cries is a "wisdom hermeneutic of cries."[12] Based on an overview of Luke/ Acts, he makes a connection between wisdom and cries in Jesus' life.

> Cries preceded Jesus' birth, accompanied it, and preceded his baptism. His ministry was one of compassion in response to the poor and suffering, and it was pervaded with the cries of demons, sufferers, opponents, disciples and crowds, and with Jesus' own cries of exultation, lamentation, or woe. The climax of his life in Jerusalem was accompanied by a crescendo of cries focused on him, and his culminating act was a loud cry from the cross as he died.[13]

The Beloved Community is the steward of the tools for discerning cries out of the cacophony. The taxonomy of moods can be used as an indicator of the health of the Beloved Community. Are all the moods present? Which mood dominates? Which mood is never heard? The Scriptures of the Old and New Testaments reflect all moods. At times, when the Beloved Community is traveling the wilderness, certain moods will take precedence. When the Beloved Community is a refuge, other moods will prevail. Because the Beloved Community is at all times and to some degree both wilderness and refuge, there is a continual white noise of the cacophony.

Within the cacophony, all cries are not created equal. Depending on the situation in the community or in the life of an individual/family in

12. Ford, *Christian Wisdom*, 45.
13. Ford, *Christian Wisdom*, 45.

the community, certain cries need to be amplified while others need to be muted. As the ears of God, the community's hermeneutic of cries, informed by the full spectrum of moods of cries, enables effective discernment. As the Beloved Community listens and discerns, it then can responsibly identify the mood that best matches the cry and provide meaning and an appropriate response. When the cries come forth, even the silent cry, the Beloved Community provides its own narrative and has at its disposal a myriad of resources—including but not limited to worship, arts, science, ethics, politics, economics, friendships, Scripture, music, liturgies, and rites and rituals.

THE BELOVED COMMUNITY AS REFUGE AND WILDERNESS: "A MIGHTY FORTRESS IS OUR GOD"

In 1998, at a tri-annual conference of Lutheran Specialized Ministers (chaplains, pastoral counselors, etc.) the keynote, "One Voice Crying in the Wilderness," was given by Dr. Frederick Niedner, a professor of Old Testament at Valparaiso University. His development of the metaphor and accompanying insights made the wilderness a primary theme in my teaching, my preaching, and my practice as a pastoral counselor. What made the image so powerful was his etymology of the word in both its Greek and Hebrew origins. As I remember his original presentation, the literal translation of the Hebrew word for wilderness is "no words." Niedner, in a recent presentation, writes:

> Stories of life and times in the wilderness run all through the Bible, and together they teach us that wilderness is a spiritual and existential place, not merely a name for geographical terrains. In particular, the wilderness sojourns of Israel and Jesus teach us that wilderness is a place in which our language, categories, and meaning-making skills fail us even as we murmur, blame, scapegoat one another, and succumb to temptations to fill the emptiness we experience with things that cannot satisfy.[14]

Niedner goes on to describe the wilderness as that ubiquitous place between freedom and bondage.

> Immigration, sobriety, abused, widowhood, orphaned or losing a child, left behind by an employer, a spouse, a community on which we depended—all departures send us into a wilderness

---

14. Niedner, "Lament and Sustenance," 2.

where our language fails, our ways of making meaning, all fail.
We want to go back, even to slavery.[15]

This places a unique responsibility on the Beloved Community in its role to normalize the wilderness. The Scriptures are written from the pervasive perspective of continual departures for places unknown, unmapped. From the first couple driven from their garden, to the desperate and fear-filled flight of Cain, to a couple fleeing to Egypt to escape a murderous tyrant, to the Son of God who had no place to lay his head, to the itinerant apostles—Scripture is the continuous epic of people encountering what might be euphemistically called "adventure" or "the frontier." In most cases, however, they found themselves bewildered in the wilderness.

In recent years, trauma theory backed by fascinating brain science has revealed a new and terrifying wilderness—the place where the wordless victim of severe abuse, war, tragedy, and natural disasters live. Combing the work of Bessel van der Kolk from a clinical perspective, Cathy Caruth's interviews, which show the importance of listening to trauma victims, and Serene Jones's book written from a pastoral and theological perspective, beloved communities have little excuse to not hear the whispered and silent cries that arise from the wilderness of those who find themselves muted to a whisper or aphasic. Van der Kolk's, Caruth's, and Jones's books—as well as other resources about trauma—indicate that the Beloved Community, or the persons within beloved communities, responsible for listening and caring, be informed and competent in being sensitive to the often disguised cry of trauma.

The best description of the complex nature and the devastating effect of trauma is Cathy Caruth's:

> Most descriptions generally agree that there is a response, sometimes delayed, to an overwhelming event or events, which takes the form of repeated, intrusive hallucinations, dreams, thoughts or behaviors stemming from the event, along with numbing that may have begun during or after the experience, and possibly also increased arousal to (and avoidance of) stimuli recalling the event. This simple definition belies a very peculiar fact: the pathology cannot be defined either by the event itself—which may or may not be catastrophic, and may not traumatize everyone equally—nor can it be defined in terms of a distortion of the event, achieving its haunting power as a result of distorting personal significances to it. The pathology consists, rather, solely in the structure of its experience or reception: the event is not

15. Niedner, "Lament and Sustenance," 8.

assimilated or experienced fully at the time, but only belatedly, in its repeated possession of the one who experiences it. To be traumatized is precisely to be possessed by an image or event.[16]

We are possessed by images. The cry of COVID—the hiss of the ventilator is a reminder of the muted cry of the intubated. The cries of public health officials offering warnings that go unheeded. If there was ever a cacophony of cries, it was in the first couple of months of the pandemic—doctors and nurses, families, essential workers crying out for help, in grief, in exhaustion. Finally, the cry of "not fair" when the wealthy and privileged went to second homes or retreated to live on their yachts.[17]

We are possessed by events. Nine minutes, twenty-nine seconds. The cry "Black Lives Matter" that finally captured the world's attention in the whispered cry of George Floyd, "I can't breathe." The cries of protest in response to Floyd's death: defund the police! The impassioned cries, chants, and responses heard from streets across the US.

Not to be overlooked are those who find themselves bewildered in the wilderness. Niedner again:

> We do well to remember that the crumbling of white supremacy, exposure of white privilege, and fall of patriarchy have cast some into a wilderness. They thought they knew the rules, the language, etc.; now they're criticized, ruled out, and damned for behaving as they always thought was their right. How do we respond to their wilderness experience?[18]

Beloved communities dare not remain silent. The temptation is to fall back to facile theodicies. One would think that the cacophony demands that God answer. Maybe. Maybe not. Beloved communities normalize the wilderness because it knows that there is finally no defense of the indefensible. Being without a working theodicy makes the response of the Beloved Community even more important. Theodicies, for the most part, are dependent on functioning closed-minded thinking. When trauma forces the failure of closed-minded thinking, theodicy fails. The poignant story of C.S. Lewis's struggle with the death of his wife chronicled in *A Grief Observed* is an illustration of how even a carefully nurtured theodicy will fail given the right trauma. In Lewis's experience, he was able to once again become a person of faith but with a disabled theodicy.

16. Caruth, *Unclaimed Experience*, 4–5.

17. My wife and I left our city which was the first Virginia community to register significant cases of COVID infections and retreated to our second home on the Sunrise Side of the Blue Ridge Mountains in central Virginia.

18. Niedner, "Lament and Sustenance," 8.

THE BELOVED COMMUNITY AS REFUGE:
NORMALIZING THE WILDERNESS

The Beloved Community is more than a place where the wilderness is normalized. It is also a place of refuge, uniquely equipped to meet the needs of those despairing who are still in the wilderness as well as those who find themselves on either side of the wilderness.

Simul justus et peccator. Among the paradoxes of Lutheran theology, the continuing tension and complementary nature of being a sinner and justified at the same time is among the most important. I argue that the beloved communities are *simul* (at the same time) wilderness and refuge.[19]

Van der Kolk writes,

> being able to feel safe with other people is probably the single most important aspect of mental health; safe connections are fundamental to meaningful and satisfying lives. Numerous studies of disaster response around the globe haves shown that social support is the most powerful protection against becoming overwhelmed by stress and trauma.[20]

Trauma theory, specifically brain science, provides the Beloved Community a conceptual framework to understand, analyze, and respond to the cacophony of cries. In the process, the Beloved Community becomes a place of safety while individuals or even most of the community may be wandering in the wilderness.

Beloved communities, properly equipped and prepared, can be a refuge. Beloved communities provide places of safety, places where the encroaching wilderness and accompanying cries with its uncertainty and its potential to disorient can be analyzed and where proper responses are made. At the first level, beloved communities provide non-reactive and empathic responses for members who find themselves under stress. A whole range of developmental yet expected transitions along the life cycle—such as chronic illness, acute illness (cancer), influenza, combining marriage and parenting with work, broken relationships, and the list goes on—are embraced by a beloved community. These challenges when encountered in isolation can be overwhelming. Life in beloved community normalizes these events and provides the care, wisdom, and hope necessary for the

---

19. With a focused self-consciousness regarding this dual nature, the Beloved Community plays a role similar to the "good enough" parent in less stressful times and the role of the "transitional" object in times of stress and disruption. See D. W. Winnicott in *Playing and Reality.*

20. van der Kolk, *The Body Keeps the Score,* 80.

person to feel "safe and secure from all alarms," as the old hymn goes. The well-prepared beloved community has at its disposal many layers of safety protocols, from the almost invisible—e.g., a kind and knowing look—to the specific and intentional—e.g., personal visits, prayer, small group support, hymns, rites.

It is at the second and third level where the resources of the Beloved Community are challenged the most. The fight/flight response is the most difficult, both for the individual and the beloved community. When the threat triggers the fight/flight response, hyper-awareness creates extreme confusion. Niedner describes the result:

> We respond to our disorientation with impatience, murmuring, rejection/suing of leaders, longing to go back, idealizing the old days, and "craving" for things we think will solve our deep hunger—plenty, certainty, longevity without fear, control (political) no matter what's necessary, even violence.[21]

While beloved communities can provide an ear for the cry of the individual who is terrorized, more serious decisions have to be made when the community itself becomes threatened. The Lutheran denomination of which I am part has its origins in a group of Saxons who, under the leadership of a charismatic pastor, chose to immigrate to the US in the first half of the nineteenth century. They fled.[22] The history of the US can be summarized: threatened by tyranny, British colonies chose to fight. The haunting image of the twentieth century is Jewish communities (beloved communities) who, when faced with the unspeakable, were immobilized, with the large majority neither fleeing nor fighting. How does a community faced with extinction make decisions?

The greatest threat to the integrity of the Beloved Community as both wilderness and refuge is the temptation to rely on simplistic platitudes when faced with crises. In the urgency of the moment, it is easy forget the broad range of resources available to the Beloved Community. The Beloved Community must be a place for the traumatized, the bereaved, the dying, the disabled, the marginalized—the last, the lost, and the least. Key for an effective response is discerning the cry in an amalgam of informed listening and intentional caring. The well-prepared beloved community is above all humbled by the cacophony of cries and its impotence to respond effectively

---

21. Niedner, "Lament and Sustenance," 11.

22. The history of the Lutheran Church Missouri Synod (LCMS) had its origins in four shiploads of immigrants who landed in New Orleans and then settled in Perry County, MO. See Forster, *Zion on the Mississippi.*

to all. Facing that reality honestly, the resulting imperative for the Beloved Community is to be intentional in building and maintaining itself.

In the conclusion of this book, I will make specific suggestions about building and maintaining the beloved community as we have described it.

PART 2

Interventions

4

What Is Beloved Community?

Jacob L. Goodson

ALL THREE OF US utilize the term "beloved community" for the purpose of diagnosing the current political divisiveness in the US and to hypothesize about the significance of this term in this current moment defined by crises, despair, and desperation. What does the term beloved community mean, and what are the attributes of such a community? To answer these two questions, I trace the term from its origins in the work of the American philosopher Josiah Royce through Martin Luther King Jr. to the recent use of the term by Joy James.

JOSIAH ROYCE ON THE BELOVED COMMUNITY

Readers met Josiah Royce in chapters 1 and 2, and I do not need to introduce any more biographical details about him except to note that part of Royce's legacy is that he coined the term "beloved community."

What are the attributes or characteristics of such a community, according to Royce? In one of his first uses of the term, Royce claims that each of us has an obligation to act as if we are bringing about such a community. He writes,

> Every proposed reform, every moral deed, is to be tested by
> whether and to what extent it contributes to the realization of
> the Beloved Community ... When one cannot find the "beloved
> community," she needs to take steps to create it and if there is
> not evidence of the existence of such a community than the rule
> to live by is To Act So As To Hasten Its Coming.[1]

We must always act in such a way as if our actions and decisions help bring about the beloved community. This functions as a Kantian-style categorical imperative within Royce's philosophy, and I find it a compelling and interesting rule. As a rule, Royce's categorical imperative can be put succinctly: always act so to bring about the coming of the beloved community.

If we follow this rule, what is it that we bring about? What does it mean to bring about the beloved community? What are the attributes or characteristics of the beloved community? According to Royce, there are five attributes or features of the beloved community. The beloved community (1) embodies universal love, (2) serves as an ideal to constantly strive toward, (3) offers a modern version of the medieval idea of the Kingdom of God, (4) requires all people to live by faith, grace, and love, and (5) represents the greatest hope possible for humanity. Royce talks about the beloved community as a universal in the sense that it ought to include all human beings and not limit itself to a particular religious community or a community only of like-minded people.

As an ideal, Royce's beloved community creates a standard for how we treat one another in our everyday lives: Are we treating others as if we are in the beloved community? Royce's other word for faith is loyalty. By loyalty, Royce means finding meaning beyond ourselves—looking to live for something greater than our own egos and self-interests. In addition to being an ideal to strive toward, Royce thinks that an actual beloved community will come about one day; this actual beloved community serves as the greatest hope we can have in terms of what humanity can be and become.

Later in the same book, Royce connects beloved community with philosophical notions of past and future. According to Royce, the beloved community is one which has a truthful memory of the past and a hopeful expectation of the future. The beloved community is a community of truthful memory in the sense that it is, in the words of Royce, a "community constituted by the fact that each of its members accepts as part of his own individual life . . . the same past events that each of his fellow-members accepts, may be called a *community of memory*."[2] To be a community of

1. Royce, *The Problem of Christianity*, 200.
2. Royce, *The Problem of Christianity*, 248.

memory means: (a) avoiding using history to justify our own self-interests, (b) being truthful about history even when doing so makes us feel uncomfortable about ourselves or our family, and (c) identifying the wounds of the past.

Beloved community is also a community of hopeful expectation. In Royce's words, a "community constituted by the fact that each of its members accepts, as part of his own individual life . . . , the same expected future events that each of his fellows accepts, may be called a *community of expectation*, or . . . a *community of hope*."[3] To be a community of hope means: (a) being oriented toward the future—more specifically, toward actualizing the beloved community, (b) being truthful about the past because beloved community cannot be achieved if there is a refusal concerning truthfulness about the past, and (c) thinking of beloved community as the achievement and embodiment of faith, hope, and love. Royce's understanding of faith, hope, and love involves his version of the Pauline cardinal virtues: loyalty to something greater than one's self (faith), hope toward the future, and universal love.[4]

These connections between community, hope, and time relate to arguments I attempted to make in the conclusion to *The Dark Years?: Philosophy, Politics, and the Problem of Predictions*.[5] In that book, I focus on the thinking of the neopragmatist philosopher, Richard Rorty—in particular, a set of predictions he makes about the twenty-first century. The conclusion concerned the development of two reasonable forms of hope in the American context: melancholic hope and redemptive hope. What is the relationship between these two forms of hope defended in the conclusion to *The Dark Years?* and Royce's emphasis on the past and future for thinking about the beloved community?

Melancholic hope relates to Royce's understanding of how the past impacts beloved community: melancholic hope involves serious and sobering recognition of America's past sins of racism and white supremacy, but also learns to become hopeful about the future of race relations in the US. Being hopeful about the future of race relations without melancholy about the past

---

3. Royce, *The Problem of Christianity*, 249.

4. Lutheran theologian Paul Hinlicky disagrees with this interpretation of Royce. Hinlicky does all he can to avoid a secular interpretation of Royce, like the one I am offering here. For instance, Hinlicky claims that Royce uses faith in line with St. Paul: for both St. Paul and Royce, "through . . . faith they enter into the promised Beloved Community by the new creative act of the Suffering Servant of the Lord on behalf of 'real, not fictitious sinners'" (Hinlicky, *Luther and the Beloved Community*, 30).

5. Goodson, *The Dark Years?*, 143–61.

and present sins of racism and white supremacy ought to be considered naïve, optimistic, and untruthful.

Redemptive hope relates to Royce's understanding of how the future helps us think about the beloved community: redemptive hope involves directing our future hopes not in politics alone, but mostly in our friendships and the relationships that constitute our everyday lives. Directing our hopes exclusively toward politics inevitably will lead to despair, disappointment, and distrust; directing our hopes to friendships and the relationships that constitute our everyday lives makes possible a hope that allows for redemption—both a redemption for ourselves and for others. Redemptive hope provides a way for us to be truthful about our personal disappointments and failures while also believing in the potential for friendships and the relationships that constitute our everyday lives to sustain our future selves. These friendships and the relationships that constitute our everyday lives represent the way that I think about what constitutes the beloved community. Later in this chapter, I return to this point in relation to Joy James's claim: "the beloved community seems to be immobilized, preoccupied with personal rather than political issues."[6]

MARTIN LUTHER KING JR. ON THE BELOVED COMMUNITY

In his doctoral program at Boston University, Martin Luther King Jr. (1929–1968) read almost all of Royce's writings. Royce was a great influence on the professors at Boston University at the time that King was a student there. Additionally, in 1956, King visited India in order to learn from and spend time with Ghandi. After King returned from India, he began using Royce's term "beloved community" to describe his reasons for remaining nonviolent as the best way to address the sins of racism and white supremacy.[7]

King was trained as an American philosopher; he told his closest friends that he wanted to be remembered as a Baptist preacher; yet, we all know him best as a civil rights leader. In the role of Baptist preacher, in April 1957, King utilizes the term "beloved community" in his sermon entitled "Birth of a New Nation":

6. James, *Seeking the Beloved Community*, 146.

7. Charles Marsh offers a brief genealogy (a genealogy we ignore in this book) of the term "beloved community" from Royce up to King: "The beloved community is . . . a 'religion of loyalty' (Royce), 'the good life of personality lived in the Beloved Community' (Randolph Bourne), or . . . the 'social egalitarianism' of Jesus Christ ([Walter] Rauschenbusch)" (Marsh, *Beloved Community*, 50).

The aftermath of nonviolence is the creation of the beloved community. The aftermath of nonviolence is redemption. The aftermath of nonviolence is reconciliation. The aftermath of violence are emptiness and bitterness. This is the thing I'm concerned about. Let us fight passionately and unrelentingly for the goals of justice and peace. But let's be sure that our hands are clean in this struggle. Let us never fight with falsehood and violence and hate and malice, but always fight with love, so that when the day comes that the walls of segregation have completely crumbled in Montgomery, that we will be able to live with people as their brothers and sisters.[8]

King offers his own characteristics of beloved community in this passage: the beloved community is one that involves justice, peace, reconciliation, redemption, truth, and turning enemies into "brothers and sisters."

This notion of turning enemies into "brothers and sisters" reflects a point that drove King throughout his career: King worried about white resentment, and he sought through nonviolence to avoid white resentment. While I admire King's conviction on this point, if we have learned anything since 2016—no matter how loving, nonviolent, peaceful, and truthful Black Lives Matter protestors behave—white resentment seems unavoidable. I agree with King that the beloved community turns enemies into "brothers and sisters," but we can no longer assume that the behavior of anti-racists will determine one way or another the resentment of racists and white supremacists.

Later in 1957, in "The Role of the Church in Facing the Nation's Chief Moral Dilemma," King uses the term again:

But the end is reconciliation; the end is redemption; the end is the creation of the beloved community. It is this type of spirit and this type of love that can transform opposers into friends. The type of love that I stress here is not *eros*, a sort of esthetic or romantic love; not *philia*, a sort of reciprocal love between personal friends; but it is *agape* which is understanding goodwill for all men. It is an overflowing love which seeks nothing in return. It is the love of God working in the lives of men. This is the love that may well be the salvation of our civilization.[9]

We often hear the claim that the ends justify the means. In this case, that would mean that the achievement of beloved community would justify getting there any way we could. King adamantly disagrees with this approach:

8. King, "Birth of a New Nation," 162.
9. King, "The Role of the Church," 190.

for King, not only is it wrong to say that the ends justify the means, but using certain means necessarily prevents ever arriving at the end goal of beloved community. For King, any approach based on hate or any approach that uses violence will block the achievement of beloved community. To achieve the end of beloved community requires the means to involve *agape* love, nonviolence, and truthfulness. According to King, beloved community represents "the salvation of our civilization."

Starting with St. Paul, there is a lengthy tradition of prioritizing *agape* love as the highest and most hopeful form of love. From Augustine through Thomas Aquinas, *agape* love remained the highest and most hopeful form of love within this tradition of Christian thought. Martin Luther King puts himself in this tradition. According to King, *agape* represents the type of love being sought within the *beloved* community. This is not surprising, given King's Baptist convictions and his commitment to Pauline theology, but it is also not surprising in relation to King's formation in American philosophy. Jonathan Edwards, C. S. Peirce, and Josiah Royce all extend the tradition of prioritizing *agape* love as the highest and most hopeful form of love; each of them do so for their own philosophical reasons. Even after King, secular philosopher Richard Rorty claims that Pauline *agape* love will serve as one of the reasons we exit what he calls the dark years from 2014 to 2045.[10]

While I admire and appreciate this aspect of the tradition of Christian thought that upholds *agape* love as the highest and most hopeful form of love, I follow Aristotle and G. W. F. Hegel in arguing for *philia* love as the most important form of love for moral and political purposes. According to Aristotle, the kind of love shared in a friendship based on virtue is *philia* love. In other words, the love often reserved for family members becomes a love shared among friends. If Martin Luther King's hopes involved being "able to live with people as their brothers and sisters," then King ought to defend *philia* love instead of *agape* love because *philia* love serves as the kind of love nurtured within family relationships. Aristotle's theory of friendship demonstrates how *philia* love can and should be extended to non-familial friendships—to those with whom we have to "be able to live with." According to Hegel, the kind of love required for responding to the indifference found within modernity is what he calls *xenophilia*—a love cultivated toward strangers as well as learning how to love the strangeness of strangers.[11] In a recent manuscript entitled *The Philosopher's Playground*, I argue that

---

10. Goodson, *The Dark Years?*, 82–93.

11. For the clearest articulation of Hegel's notion of *xenophilia*, see Shanks, *Hegel vs. "Inter-faith Dialogue,"* 37–66.

Hegelian *xenophilia* serves as the best possible philosophical response to the problem of *xenophobia*.[12] Of course, the problem of *xenophobia* serves as one of the driving forces for the extreme political divisiveness we currently see in the US. *Agape* love allows us to love others, but the limitations of *agape* love in relation to the problem of *xenophobia* concerns how such a love remains driven by our own motivation relating to goodwill. *Xenophilia*, on the other hand, requires us to love others on their terms. *Philia* love turns non-family members into relationships with a bond like family; *xenophilia* achieves this without requiring friends to be like us because we come to love the otherness and strangeness of our friends. In chapter 6, Kuehnert defends and talks about this aspect of beloved community under the concept of differentiation.

One final question concerning Martin Luther's King's use of the term, beloved community: What are the differences between King and Royce on the beloved community? In his book, entitled *Beloved Community*, Charles Marsh draws a strong contrast between King's and Royce's uses of beloved community. Marsh claims:

> In using the term "beloved community," King borrowed from a discourse which had been fashionable in American philosophical and theological circles throughout the early and middle twentieth century. Most of these formulations, however, had the effect of reducing transcendence to some mode or modulation of human experience, or of describing beloved community as an inevitable historical achievement. The influential philosopher Josiah Royce spoke of beloved community as "a perfectly lived unity of individual men joined in one divine chorus," and gave voice to the essence of Protestant ethical religion; the beloved community shimmers with liberal hopes of human progress and perfectibility . . .
>
> But in King's hands, the idea of beloved community was invigorated with theological vitality and moral urgency, so that the prospects of social progress came to look less like an evolutionary development and more like a divine gift . . . God remains [for King] from beginning to end the ultimate agent of human liberation, not only in America but throughout all nations and in creation . . . [B]eloved community depends on a theological, one might say ecclesiological, *event*. In other words, the brotherhood and sisterhood of humankind radiates out from the fellowship of the faithful . . . Thus, the beloved community is the new social space of reconciliation introduced into history

12. Goodson, *The Philosopher's Playground*, ch. 7.

by the Church . . . The beloved community is not shaped finally by a "religion of loyalty" (Royce) . . . ; rather, the beloved community is established by the "great *event* on Calvary," "the great *event* that stands at the center of [Christian] faith which reveals to us that God is on the side of truth and love and justice," as King explained in his Dexter sermon, "Paul's Letter to American Christianity."[13]

Marsh is right that King's use of beloved community ought to be judged as deeply and substantively theological, whereas Royce's original use of the term remains humanist, philosophical, and universal in scope.

JOY JAMES ON SEEKING THE BELOVED COMMUNITY

Originally published in the first volume of the journal *Trans-Scripts*, Joy James includes her essay, entitled "Black Suffering in Search of the 'Beloved Community,'" in a collection of essays published as *Seeking the Beloved Community: A Feminist Race Reader*. James currently serves as the Presidential Professor of Humanities at Williams College in Williamstown, Massachusetts. In her essay, James builds on Martin Luther King's use of the term "beloved community." I end with James's reflections on the term because she offers both a defense and strong critique of it.

In defense of the term, Joy James links it with death and despair. She claims, "Political resistance could kill you, well actually the state could in response to your resistance, but the beloved community could save you."[14] This claim comes in the context of James making a case for a "mandate for nonviolent civil disobedience,"[15] and her point is not that the beloved community will save one's life from the state, but rather the beloved community saves one "from meaningless death and despair."[16] In this sense, the beloved community "save[s]" those who participate in "nonviolent civil disobedience" because the risk of this political resistance includes both death and despair.[17] Although a beloved community cannot save one's life from the lethal power of the state, the beloved community can provide meaning for their death. A beloved community can "save" one from despair while living

---

13. Marsh, *Beloved Community*, 49–50.

14. James, *Seeking the Beloved Community*, 145.

15. See James, *Seeking the Beloved Community*, 144–46.

16. James, *Seeking the Beloved Community*, 145.

17. See James, *Seeking the Beloved Community*, 144–46.

through political oppression.[18] James, therefore, seems to agree with King's claim that beloved community represents "the salvation of our civilization."[19]

Offering a strong critique of the term "beloved community," Joy James further reflects on why the beloved community cannot in fact save one's life from the lethal power of the state. She writes, "So, the beloved community seems to be immobilized, preoccupied with personal rather than political issues, avoiding a conversation about and with the dead."[20] With this reflection, James points out the impotence of the beloved community when it comes to actual dead bodies—especially actual dead Black bodies. Black bodies suffer and die because of the lethal power of the state; the beloved community neither saves them nor mobilizes a response to their deaths afterward.

I appreciate Joy James connecting the term "beloved community" with the question and reality of death. I agree with her that the beloved community, as a philosophical ideal for what a community can be or might become, cannot and does not save actual lives. Also, though, I think it appropriate (with James) to emphasize how beloved community might provide ways of dealing with one's despair—especially in relation to being in a context of political oppression. Providing responses to despair seems a much more realistic expectation for the beloved community than providing responses to actual deaths. This will be an argument I pick up in chapter 8, building from the wisdom of Brad Elliot Stone's interpretation of James Baldwin's work.

On the one hand, Joy James is exactly right that the beloved community seems more "personal rather than political."[21] Perhaps this point is reflected in my argument concerning redemptive hope—that hope ought to be placed much more in our everyday personal relationships rather than in American politics or even a particular political party. On the other hand: if the ideals of the Roycean beloved community come to fruition, then the beloved community would serve as a kind of necessary judgment against political oppression and any and all suffering caused by politics. The beloved community encourages and inspires us to listen for and to the cries of the wounded in relation to political oppression.

18. See James, *Seeking the Beloved Community*, 145.
19. See King, "The Role of the Church," 190.
20. James, *Seeking the Beloved Community*, 146.
21. James, *Seeking the Beloved Community*, 146.

CONCLUSION: HOPE AND BELOVED COMMUNITY

I have written a lot on hope and less on community.[22] Part of the reason for that is that communities tend to be difficult and messy. I often hear philosophers and theologians assert that "We should begin with community" or "The community is what gives meaning to individual experience." While I do not disagree with these claims, I often find that those defending the priority of community do not give us realistic pictures of how communities function and what communities look like. I write less on community because I do not want to be accused of falling into this same trap.

What I find compelling about Royce's, King's, and Joy James's notions of beloved community, however, is that all three think through the messiness of community. Joy James connects the beloved community with the reality of death and despair, making her argument all about the messiness of community and personal relationships. King recognizes that cultivating a community with both Black and white people together comes with its wounds. In fact, Charles Marsh claims that King's notion of "beloved community remains broken and scattered, [only] an eschatological hope, yet precisely a hope that intensifies rather than absolves us from responsibilities in the here and now."[23] Royce turns the beloved community into a universal, which sounds like it might not take seriously the messiness, but he does so in order to treat community as an ideal that helps us manage and negotiate the communities of which we participate in our everyday lives. The way that ideal helps us is that it offers a rule in our everyday lives: always act in such a way as if our actions and decisions help bring about the beloved community. Such a rule does not ignore the messiness of living in community but, in fact, helps us get through the messiness by maintaining our integrity in the relationships most challenging to us.

If I were to write more on community beyond this chapter, I would take the following approach: we must take into account the ways that communities involve broken promises and yet trust, conflict and disappointment, forgiveness and recognition. Communities give us both surprising friendships and failed relationships. Communities constantly exclude and include without much reason given for either exclusion or inclusion, and one of the ways to contribute to community concerns calling out the exclusion of those who have less power and no voice within a particular community. Calling out those with social capital, however, means accepting that conflict and tension will arise and will continue within that community.

22. Goodson, *Strength of Mind*, chs. 8–10; see Goodson, *The Dark Years?*, 143–61; see Goodson and Stone, *Introducing Prophetic Pragmatism*, ch. 5.

23. Marsh, *Beloved Community*, 50.

Thinking of communities in terms of how they allow for both contradictions and ideals—broken promises, conflict, disappointment but also forgiveness, recognition, and trust—becomes one way to say that we maintain hope in and strive toward the beloved community.

5

Avoiding Idealism with Beloved Communities

Brad Elliott Stone

USING A PROPHETIC PRAGMATIST framework, this chapter seeks to avoid idealism when discussing beloved communities. The notion of the beloved community is often used as a description of *the ideal* community—singular and Platonic, freed from the messiness of concrete struggle and individual interests, an end goal that can be achieved. This depiction of beloved communities is ironic insofar as it is often presented as a consequence of pragmatism. Although Martin Luther King Jr. is not usually counted among the pragmatists, Royce is indeed canonized as one of the classical pragmatists. Yet Royce's absolute idealism is distinctive compared to the overall movement of pragmatism and antithetical compared to the neopragmatism of Richard Rorty and Cornel West. How must a beloved community be described given my neopragmatist commitments to antirealism, antifoundationalism, and the decentralization of the subject?

FROM IDEALISM TO MATERIALISM

Pragmatism is often seen as a critique of idealism (be it absolute, subjective, or transcendental). "Faith requires us to be materialists without flinching," C. S. Peirce tells us in his summation of the unwritten chapter 9 of "A Guess at the Riddle."[1] Of course, materialism refers to both *physicalism*, the belief that all entities are strictly an arrangement of physical "stuff" (with no room for nonphysical or mental "stuff"), and a view about the relationship between subjects and objects—in short, a view that sees subjects as simply one more kind of object. Since idealism needs the separation of subject and object (whether or not it denies physicalism), it is the latter sense of materialism we will explore here. That said, the first sense of materialism grounds the second one in important ways.

Although West's 1977 article, "Philosophy and the Afro-American Experience," already addressed antifoundationalism and historicism, his 1980 dissertation, published in 1991 as *The Ethical Dimensions of Marxist Thought*, locates in Marx a critique of idealism and an embrace of materialism. West's emphasis on radical historicism in Marx seeks to separate Marx from the dominant forms of Marxism that fail to heed Marx's historicism and return to the foundationalist quest for (objective and idealistic) certainty. West starts the dissertation with two important claims about radical historicism: (1) "the radical historicist sees the dynamic historical processes as subjecting all criteria, grounds, and foundations to revision and modification," and (2) "the only plausible candidates for the criteria, grounds, or foundations in question would be the *contingent, community-specific* agreements people make in relation to particular norms, aims, goals, and objectives."[2] There are no ahistorical foundations for our morals or even theoretical knowledge, nor are there systems of thought that are settled once and for all. As time passes, communities are not only falsifying past truths and holding as true things once unthought or deemed false, but the very criteria and processes of evaluation are changing historically.

According to West, "The point is not to lift oneself out of the flux of history—an impossible task—but rather to immerse oneself more deeply into history by consciously identifying with—and digesting *critically* the values of—a particular community or tradition."[3] If one were to wish to continue speaking of foundations, criteria, seats of philosophical judgment, and "objective" "standards," one would have to grant such power to one's

---

1. Peirce, "A Guess at the Riddle," 354.
2. West, *The Ethical Dimensions of Marxist Thought*, 1.
3. West, *The Ethical Dimensions of Marxist Thought*, 3.

own historical situatedness in a concrete, equally historically situated community. Philosophy refuses to grant this fact, deeming such a position to be relativist. West, in the spirit of his professor and mentor Richard Rorty, rejects the label of relativism, asserting that even the philosophical notions and distinctions (especially the very notion of relativism) are themselves simply practices agreed to by a particular, contingent, historically situated community. Given that this community has not been very helpful or useful to the cause of Black liberation, there is no reason to blindly follow such practices, especially when one is repeatedly reminded that one is not a member of such a community by centuries of racist philosophers. Thus historicism is a *metaphilosophical* position, a position about what philosophy is and is not and what philosophy can or cannot do. The acceptance of radical historicism as one's metaphilosophical position leads one to be no longer attracted to "the vision of philosophy as the quest for philosophical certainty, the search for philosophic foundations."[4]

West's dissertation then presents an account of how Marx became disenchanted with philosophy, followed by an analysis of Marx's own radical historicism, beginning with Marx's 1845 *Theses on Feuerbach*. It is here that West begins to explore the tensions between materialism and idealism. West discerns that Marx's understanding of materialism is different from traditional, mere physicalist, accounts.

> Materialists have tended to ignore the activity or practices of human beings because their mechanistic (and often deterministic) models of causation assume the human mind to be merely passive, to be solely the receptor of outside stimuli. It was left to the idealists, e.g., Kant, Fichte, Reinhold, Hegel, to stress the activity of the mind, the human contribution to knowing. Armed with its own set of anticipations, assumptions, categories, and aims, the mind, for the idealist, transforms and transcends that which is "given" to it or that which it confronts. Knowing is a struggle between the obstinate object and active subject. But the idealists conceive human beings solely as subjects of knowing, mere bearers of self-consciousness. They ignore the material side of people, their natural needs and social interest.[5]

For West, Marx's materialism fixes the problem of material passivity while also grounding the knowing subject on earth. It breaks down the obstinacy, the ob-ject-ivity, the being thrown-against, the *Gegen-stand*, of the world in which people live and exist. The distinction between subject and object

---

4. West, *The Ethical Dimensions of Marxist Thought*, 12.
5. West, *The Ethical Dimensions of Marxist Thought*, 64.

breaks down due to material needs being met with human agency, which is itself material. In this sense, thought is one more material moment of the universe.

One key consequence of Marx's materialism is that our pursuit of solutions to material problems will themselves be material instead of an idealistic utopia that happens somewhere in the noumenal realm, detached from matter and actual practical concerns. Instead, thought is an activity that takes place in an active material world, and our thinking is not merely an act of description but of modification: "The philosophers have only *interpreted* the world in various ways; the point, however, is to *change* it."[6]

Having explicated Marx's radical historicism and materialism, West spends the remaining chapters of the book commenting on Marxist positions that return to the old philosophical model in the hope of gaining certainty or foundations. He highlights three key figures: Engels, Kautsky, and Lukács. Each one gets their own chapter. In the chapter on Kautsky, West writes the following about materialism and idealism.

> Kautsky compares [his] materialist approach to the idealist approach. The latter arises, he claims, from a dissatisfaction with the former. Specifically, the idealist approach holds that the materialist approach does not explain or cannot account for the strong sense of obligation people feel toward the moral law, and especially in those cases where it seems highly unlikely that moral duties, such as self-sacrifice, come from rational self-interested hedonistic calculation. This dissatisfaction results in a contempt for the contingency and mutability of nature (including human nature) and yields a search for absolutes and timeless moral truths. This idealistic approach arrives at the view that the moral law is of supernatural origin; this approach then begins to work out a proof for the existence of a supernatural world.[7]

Given West's focus on ethics in his dissertation, this passage shows the key tension between materialism and idealism. The idealist has sincere doubts about whether moral obligations will be accepted by people. As a result, they seek to circumvent human nature and establish necessary and immutable laws of morality. These laws are not laws of nature (or else freedom would be compromised), so they have to create a supernatural or noumenal world *where* such law reigns. This is why there is such a worry about moral relativism: the fact that different communities at different times have

---

6. Marx and Engels, *Collected Works*, 6; cited by West, *The Ethical Dimensions of Marxist Thought*, 68; emphasis West's.

7. West, *The Ethical Dimensions of Marxist Thought*, 120.

different ethical norms and moral expectations threatens the utopian quest for certainty. The materialist, historicist, and pragmatist response is to see morality as a strictly human affair, historically bounded and grounded on the concrete practices of everyday people.

Although the idealist will claim that their objective, ahistorical moral views are universal, they are actually quite particular, namely, ideologies of a particular class, race, or nation. For West (along with Marx and Kautsky), universal claims about morality are actually illusory expressions of hope that one's own moral view would be everyone's view. Idealists wish to shed themselves of the burden of history and custom. As West writes, "the materialist approach is superior to the idealist approach because it does not posit illusory entities to account for why human beings take moral laws seriously . . . the materialist approach . . . confines people to their sense experiences and claims that ethical matters should be restricted to the exercise of the natural faculties of people."[8] It is important to highlight that West is not suggesting that morality itself is an illusion, just the idealist notion that there is some ultimate guarantor of the universality of moral claims. The materialist's argument is not that there is no such thing as morality; rather, it is the claim that the justifications of a community's moral system is itself part of that community: a set of values, particular goals the community seeks to achieve, and other beliefs held by the community in question.

Thus, the pragmatist prefers a notion of beloved community that does not point to some other realm where things are ideal. King's formulation of the beloved community is actually simply a view about the Kingdom of God brought to earth, which, qua Western theological position, is an idealist one. Similarly, Royce's absolute idealism seeks to determine the ideal grounds for beloved community instead of transforming his communities from within. West is aware of Royce's concern—the hope for ultimate justification—but it does not inspire due to its lack of courage to tackle problems of community formation and modification in the full messiness of matter. Thus, West says about Royce's absolute idealism,

> I suspect that something deeper is going on. Royce believes more is at stake than warding off willful subjectivism and epistemic relativism. Reality and truth must, in some sense, be absolute not only because skepticism lurks about, but also—and more important, because it is the last and only hope for giving meaning to the strenuous mood, for justifying the worthwhileness of our struggle to endure . . . he holds on for dear life.[9]

8. West, *The Ethical Dimensions of Marxist Thought*, 121.

9. West, *Keeping Faith*, 116.

West's answer to Royce would entail a conversation about how to decide whether something is worthwhile, about what needs to be held on for dear life, about what matters for a given, historically situated community facing particular problems. One does not need to be an idealist in order to decide these issues.

In fairness, I suspect pragmatism's critique of idealism is more due to idealism's critique of materialism, discounting non-idealist positions as relativism. Yet, the claim of relativism requires the presupposition that there are truths that are external to concrete communities, often located in a place that is externally far away from the world in which we find ourselves. Once one denies that presupposition, the charge of relativism becomes less venomous. So the question is whether or not there is a choice between idealism and materialism when it comes to dealing with, in this context, beloved communities. I do not believe that an idealist who participates in a beloved community automatically becomes a bad member of such a community. Does the idealist feel the same way about materialists?

FROM OBJECTIVITY TO SOLIDARITY

Richard Rorty was a strong influence on Cornel West. Rorty's historicism undergirds West's historicism: "Rorty's historicist turn was like music to my ears—nearly as sweet as The Dramatics, The Spinners, or the Main Ingredient, whom I then listened to daily for sanity."[10] Rorty's critique of idealism influenced West's embrace of materialism, so I do not repeat the argument here.[11] In Rorty's second major book, *Contingency, Irony, and Solidarity*, Rorty argues for the possibility of moral progress without an objective standard against which such progress would be measured. This section focuses on Rorty's understanding of solidarity, and why it might be preferable to idealist accounts of humanity or human nature.

Rorty had already discussed solidarity as an alternative to objectivity in 1985 and 1987. Rorty begins the essay "Solidarity or Objectivity?" by comparing the two.

> There are two principle ways in which reflective human beings try, by placing their lives in a larger context, to give sense to those lives. The first is by telling the story of their contribution to a community. This community may be the actual historical one in which they live, or another actual one, distant in time or

10. West, *The Ethical Dimensions of Marxist Thought*, xx.

11. Cf. Rorty, *Consequences of Pragmatism*, esp. ch. 8; *Philosophy and the Mirror of Nature*, esp. chs. 6 and 8.

place, or a quite imaginary one, consisting perhaps of a dozen heroes and heroines selected from history or fiction or both. The second way is to describe themselves as standing in immediate relation to a nonhuman reality. This relation is immediate in the sense that it does not derive from a relation between such a reality and their tribe, or their nation, or their imagined band of comrades. I shall say that stories of the former kind exemplify the desire for solidarity, and that stories of the latter kind exemplify the desire for objectivity. Insofar as a person is seeking solidarity, she does not ask about the relation between the practices of the chosen community and something outside that community. Insofar as she seeks objectivity, she distances herself from the actual persons around her not by thinking of herself as a member of some other real or imaginary group, but rather by attaching herself to something which can be described without reference to any particular human beings.[12]

At the heart of solidarity, Rorty argues, is the sense of community that grounds the choices one makes. Even if one does not wish to choose their own community, they can connect to some other community that will perhaps offer respite. Objectivity is the detachment from any community, to step outside of one's own humanity. Notice that Rorty's concern is that objectivity denies the fundamental role of communities (even if they are fictitious) to human thought and action. Even fictional communities (dare I suggest fictional beloved communities?) are better than idealist objectivity. Rorty argues in the essay that objectivity as a philosophical goal actually comes from a particular community: the idealist community of "contemporary European life . . . nurtured by the Enlightenment."[13] As shown above, West makes a similar argument: there is an actual historical community (which I may or may not wish to be part of) whose habits of inquiry abstracts away those very community underpinnings. One must ask (1) what purpose objectivity serves such a community compared to alternatives, and (2) whether one must be a member of such a community or whether one can exercise one's right to exit.[14]

Rorty continues this theme in the 1987 essay, "Science as Solidarity." Observing that objectivity is a habit "of a secularized culture in which the scientist replaces the priest,"[15] Rorty explores whether science should be treated like a kind of religion. Unfortunately, the history of philosophy

12. Rorty, *Objectivity, Relativism, and Truth*, 21.
13. Rorty, *Objectivity, Relativism, and Truth*, 28.
14. For more on "right to exit," cf. Appiah, *The Ethics of Identity*, ch. 2.
15. Rorty, *Objectivity, Relativism, and Truth*, 35.

follows this power shift, leaving philosopher-as-priest to become philosopher-as-scientist. Science, Rorty reminds us, is not "objective" in the philosophical sense at all. Rather, science serves as an example of solidarity. *Philosophy and the Mirror of Nature* also explores this theme: it could be said that philosophers often try to out-science scientists. Scientists, contrary to idealist philosophers, have grounded their claims on a notion of solidarity, not objectivity. Scientific truths are truths as held by the scientific community, a concrete network of laboratories, theorists, students, etc. Theories are crafted and tested in order to explain a given phenomenon, but new data can always change the theory, even to the point of falsification. Thus, science does not seek eternal, necessary truths. Its purpose is functional instead of descriptive. Science is always on the lookout for a better way of explaining phenomena and predicting new possibilities. This is the only way, Rorty argues, our society should model itself like science. Is science a beloved community? Yes.

In *Contingency, Irony, and Solidarity*, we see Rorty's application of solidarity to social-political philosophy. In the final chapter, "Solidarity," Rorty doubles down on the centrality of the three contingencies addressed in the first part of the book: language, self, and community. Because of these contingencies, there is no way to use notions like *inhuman* to describe the Nazis. This would presuppose that somehow people were not what they were. The truth is that all events in human history, be they positive or negative, are possible as free human actions. How can we morally judge the actions of Nazis if there is no objective notion of justice or code of ideal moral behavior?

Rorty believes we can judge Nazis based on the failure of German thinking that ought to have led them to behave differently. What was this failure of German thinking? The very idea that there is something called human nature that endows all human beings with something called dignity that was inalienable and morally good. The Nazis simply replaced that with "that person is a Jew." It turns out that idealism does not help much when it comes to stopping the killing of six million people.[16] This grand idealist notion of human nature was unable to ground the solidarity needed between Jewish and non-Jewish Germans. Meanwhile, Rorty points out, Danes and Italians were more likely to find solidarity with Jews, not as fellow human beings but in terms of occupation, region, and other things that seem less significant than the notion of human nature.

16. Goodson highlights this issue in his presentation of Joy James's response to the notion of the beloved community (see ch. 4).

Morality does not need the necessity that idealists suggest is necessary for effectiveness. As Rorty writes, "a belief can still regulate action, can still be thought worth dying for, among people who are quite aware that this belief is caused by nothing deeper than contingent historical circumstance."[17] These beliefs would be community-held beliefs that motivate action qua part of the life of a given community. If we enlarge our notion of community, we will be more sensitive to the suffering of others (usually those considered as non-members of the community) and find points of similarity that can serve as the grounds for solidarity. This notion of morality places the moral criterion at the local level. We often morally fail locally instead of at the level of the idealist moral law. Rorty uses America as a poignant example.

> Consider, as a final example, the attitude of contemporary American liberals to the unending hopelessness and misery of the lives of the young blacks in American cities. Do we say that these people must be helped because they are our fellow human beings? We may, but it is much more persuasive, morally as well as politically, to describe them as our fellow *Americans*—to insist that it is outrageous that an *American* should live without hope. The point of these examples is that our sense of solidarity is strongest when those with whom solidarity is expressed are thought of as "one of us," where "us" means something smaller and more local than the human race.[18]

One cannot simply suggest that one has a moral duty to someone else purely due to the other person being a human being. The consequence historically has been to claim that the other is somehow not a human being at all, even if they are human in appearance (Jews in Germany, Africans in America). However, once Black people are seen as fellow American citizens instead of ahistorical people from nowhere, one can ask whether America wants citizens to face such indecent levels of injustice. Racism in the US is wrong, not because it violates some cosmic code of human dignity, but because it violates the rights of citizens. These rights, of course, are themselves not cosmic; we agreed to treat American citizens a particular way, so when we do not, we have violated not the universal moral law but the rules of our own community. Of course, even the national level might be too large to ground solidarity. It might simply be sharing a hobby or enjoying the same books. By rooting solidarity into concrete communities instead of abstract universal ones, one can cultivate the correct moral feelings that will achieve

17. Rorty, *Contingency, Irony, and Solidarity*, 189.
18. Rorty, *Contingency, Irony, and Solidarity*, 191.

our goal (for Rorty, the political goal is simply the minimization of suffering, humiliation, and pain).

Solidarity is at the heart of beloved communities. Beloved communities are non-universal communities of "us" that seek to live together in a certain way to bring about certain public goals. The ground for such solidarity cannot be abstract; it has to be named in such a way that all of its members see themselves connected in that way concretely (vs. mere membership in an abstract class of objects). Beloved communities are plural in this sense. Every "us" is, as it were, a proper subset of humanity. Idealism hates this fact, but Rorty wonders what kind of evidence would show that human behavior is so fundamentally broken such that we behave in the ways that we do.

VOLUNTARISM, FALLIBILISM, AND EXPERIMENTALISM

In his essay, "Pragmatism and the Sense of the Tragic," already discussed in chapter 2, West highlights three "principal philosophic slogans" of American pragmatism: voluntarism, fallibilism, and experimentalism.[19] I will argue in this section that beloved communities are to be understood as voluntary, fallible, experimental groups of people, gathered to address specific problems and achieve specific, concrete goals.

Voluntarism for West includes two theses. First, "truth is a species of the good" or "our beliefs about the way the world is have ethical significance."[20] This is an application of the pragmatic maxim formulated by Peirce: our claims about the world have consequences, and we are to judge the truth of those claims in light of their practical consequences. Hence, to say that some proposition is true is to state that the content of the proposition furthered some goal or situation. The second thesis follows from the first. Since truth is a species of the good, the future becomes the time when truth is known: "the good is defined in relation to temporal consequences."[21] We will understand it better by and by, as the old song goes.

For both of these theses, we have a wonderful pragmatist understanding of the future. West writes that "the future has ethical significance . . . the key to pragmatism . . . is its emphasis on the ethical significance of the future."[22] As West reminds us in the song "3Ms" on the *Sketches from My Culture* album, "history is incomplete, the future is open-ended, what we do

19. West, *Keeping Faith*, 109.
20. West, *Keeping Faith*, 110.
21. West, *Keeping Faith*, 110.
22. West, *Keeping Faith*, 111.

can and will make a difference!"[23] Indeed, West argues that "human will can make the future different and, possibly, better relative to human ends and aims."[24] Of course, this is the pragmatist notion of meliorism, that actions can improve current situations, and that thinking involves seeking new possibilities that will make a better future possible.

The consequence of this voluntarism, West argues, is fallibilism and experimentalism. Since goals changes—and thus the good changes—so then would truth change. Something might have been held as true in the past, but the present situation may need a different solution or a different outcome. Thus, something may now be "more true" than the earlier truth. In some cases, the "truth" turns out now to be "false." Fallibilism is the willingness to hold beliefs today in full awareness that they might be false tomorrow as we gain new information. Fallibilism is a safeguard against dogmatism and conformity. Experimentalism is the willingness to try new things in response to new situations and problems. Combined with fallibilism, we get a scenario where people try to solve problems through imaginative new ideas and actions.

One statement by West serves as a perfect definition of a beloved community for the sake of this chapter: "Unique selves acting in and through participatory communities give ethical significance to an open, risk-ridden future."[25] Beloved communities are experimental, fallible, and voluntarist. They decide that whatever the future holds becomes more durable, more experiential, if approached together. Beloved communities are communities of the future, not of the past. I worry that many who now attempt to form beloved communities try to form King's beloved community. That would be a past community. We need a community that is looking into today's future, so it might be quite different than King's ideal of beloved community.

PRACTICING BELOVED COMMUNITY

In this chapter, I have outlined a materialist critique of an idealism that gets in the way of creating beloved communities. I conclude by giving *practical* advice about how to avoid idealism in our beloved communities.

There are three important things to keep in mind here so as not to fall into the trap of sentimental idealism when we talk about beloved community. First, we must stay vigilantly aware that a beloved community cannot come about by political means alone. The inverse must be true: once a

23. Cf. West, *Sketches from My Culture*.

24. West, *Keeping Faith*, 111.

25. West, *Keeping Faith*, 113.

beloved community is established, it will have a clear political agenda. One cannot vote a beloved community into existence. Second, we must avoid the temptation to reduce a beloved community to some set of economic programs as if poverty is the barrier to access to a beloved community. Instead, once a beloved community is established, everyone will be acutely aware of the needs of others, thus spurring new models of economics. Finally, one must not assume that everyone *must* be in a beloved community. That there are some who would rather quarrel or be divisive should not keep a beloved community from forming. If there is a beloved community, and one would rather not be part of it, they are to be allowed the right to exit. Thus, a beloved community is neither a compromise between factions nor a reconciliation of different political stances. It is a commitment to care about others and do concrete actions for each other for the sake of being a community.

Let us explore briefly, by sake of contrast, what a beloved community cannot be. A beloved community cannot be a global phenomenon. It is inherently local. One of the problems currently facing us is the drive to make everything *global*. Although this goal sounds noble, it is often the result of neoliberal capitalism (neoliberalism, for short), which turns the world into one homogeneous place such that particular goods and services would have a worldwide appeal, audience, and set of consumers. Let us call this drive *globalization*. The idea of a global unity, often at the expense of local unities that make the world heterogeneous, demands a kind of *conformity* that could only be enforced with political authoritarianism and economic sanctions, neither of which has room for the real engines of a beloved community, love, and community. When we realize that the world can be composed of a plurality of beloved communities, even ones quite different than the ones in which we participate, the global concerns begin to melt somewhat. Every beloved community is local, connected to the individuals who live in them. Although I can claim that I seek beloved community with people I do not know, I could never actually realize such a community.

A beloved community cannot be a national phenomenon. Nationalism, and its affiliated concept of patriotism, hinders a beloved community because, once again, it relies on a kind of conformity that is never present. A beloved community is a principle, not an *argumentum ad populum*. A beloved community does not belong to any particular political party, religion, or racial group. A beloved community has no ideology except that love is sufficient for community-building. A beloved community is not interested in membership rosters, followers on Twitter, or any other indicator of "influence." It is a deliberate effort by deliberate people to live deliberate lives together towards deliberate goals. In today's society, "membership" is valued at the expense of service, connection, obligation, etc. Also on the rise is slacktivism, the ability to simply sign on to movements without any actual connection between the people involved. A beloved community means that I can call on you—the one I know can do X—to do X while I—the one everyone else in the community knows can do Y—to do Y. There is no beloved community in which a given individual can passively be a member. Everyone in a beloved community bears gifts that are freely given to the community. A beloved community is indeed a local phenomenon, and one can be in multiple beloved communities.

Following the principal slogans of pragmatism, here are three features of beloved communities that keep them from falling into the traps aforementioned:

1. Beloved communities are *voluntary* (in the philosophical sense of voluntarism). "Whosoever will . . ." is Jesus' phrasing of voluntarism (Rev 22:17). No one can be forced into such a community, nor can anyone be forced to stay in one. beloved communities require a *willingness*, a *voluntas*, that animates the working together of individuals.

2. Beloved communities are *fallible*. A beloved community has nothing figured out *a priori* to action. When something does not work, a beloved community changes its views and subsequent actions. It does not seek certainty but community. It is not interested in being right. It is interested in whether everyone knows each other, whether everyone is vulnerable to the events of those in the community.

3. Beloved communities are *experimental*. They seek to move us to unknown territory, new possibilities of living together, new ways to address old problems. A beloved community has a kind of nimbleness that resists old styles of codification. Beloved communities are communities of *inquiry* that consistently ask "What if we were to . . . ?" with full awareness that tomorrow brings new ideas. The commitment is not to "victory" but to staying together, to seeing an issue or struggle through, to sharing joys and sorrows.

Thus, a beloved community cannot be an idealist vision. It is a pragmatic, historical, local effort that seeks to edify life together in a world of monadic individualism.

6

The Marriage of Idealism and Materialism

Philip R. Kuehnert

How good and pleasant it is when brothers live together in unity! (Ps 133:1)

CASE STUDIES

In my training as a pastoral psychotherapist, case studies were a primary mode of learning. Both audio taping of sessions and verbatims (dialogue between therapist and client painstakingly recreated) were expected for both individual and group supervision. Careful attention was focused on the conversations between therapist and client regarding its helpfulness or lack of same. In addition, this process was carefully considered through the lens of the particular theory of therapy used. In seeking certification for levels of competence, detailed case studies were prepared that included all of the above and were presented to a panel of adjudicators who then engaged the candidate in lengthy conversation.

Although not named case studies, it is the stories of individuals, families, communities, and cultures that provide the insights and eventually theories as to why they either thrive or fail. Freud's famous case histories of Rat

Man, Wolf Man, and Little Hans are still reference points in psychoanalysis. Margaret Mead's study in Oceana of preliterate people produced fascinating books in which she postulated and defended her theories. Recently, it was reading Amy Chugh's *The Person You Mean to Be* that made me think differently about the present project. Chugh's intention is to bring science and stories together with her stated purpose to move her readers from believers to builders. Throughout the book, she explores the relationship between science and stories, acknowledging the inherent human urge to move from thought (idealism) to action (materialism). The challenge here is how to mine and refine the rich ore of philosophical thought so that the beauty (truth) of the resulting pure metal and finally the beauty of the resulting jewelry can be enjoyed by the unsophisticated eye. Chugh is one of several writers who today are attempting to popularize deep thinking, academic research, and data by weaving the underlying philosophy/science/anthropology/theology in narratives that are gripping (spellbinding) by the nature of the struggle, drama, or obstacles described.[1]

For Chugh's book (and for this book), the word "building" is the nitroglycerin. The intentional use of this word edges us toward a battlefield littered with the debris and skeletal remains of many failed efforts to create a community where love, equality, equity, inclusion, and diversity reign. We claim to be intrepid without apology as we venture forth into this much visited battlefield. We up the ante intentionally as we invoke the adjective *beloved* for the concept of *community*. Maybe, just maybe, the insights of the idealism as explicated by Jacob Goodson and the materialism of Brad Elliott Stone combined with the spiritual grounding of religious traditions from Islam, Judaism, and Christianity may produce, if not a basic recipe for communities where love, equality, equity, inclusion, and diversity reign, at least an architectural template. We believe that we are not alone in our desire to offer our creativity and energy to humbly create a better, safer, and more sustainable world.

I see this book as an effort to combine philosophy (the ideal) with stories (the material). Admittedly anecdotal, I witnessed Goodson's and Stone's presentations capture the attention and energize a group of exhausted participants who had been on a Zoom screen for four plus hours. The energizing catalyst was their presentations that did just that—combined their philosophical reasoning with their stories. That is not new, of course, nor is it new when it comes to the effort to create communities. There has been no lack of ideals for community and certainly no lack of attempts to realize

1. Others are George Lakoff's *Don't Think of an Elephant: Know Your Values and Frame the Debate,* as well as Jonathan Haidt's *The Righteous Mind: Why Good People are Divided by Politics and Religion.*

the ideal. Thus, the battlefield littered with the debris and skeletal remains of failed attempts.

Within religious communities and, in particular, when considering the goal (ideal) of a better community, there are many case studies (books, seminars, workshops) of how religious beliefs have given rise to "meeting together" (Heb 10:25). The thriving religious publishing business gives proof that people who commit themselves to meeting together are looking for new and better ways. Many of these success stories are shamelessly marketed as "the way" to do it better. The church-growth movement in the last two decades of the last century exploited this desire with few results that proved sustainable.

In this chapter, I intend to do three things. First, using Brad Elliott Stone's prescription about the beloved community as local, voluntary, fallible, experimental, and with an exit option, I will present a case study of my experience with what became *my* beloved community in the Tidewater area of Virginia. Second, I will present a second case study from my pastoral experience in Atlanta, titled "The Waste Howling Wilderness." Finally, I will critically examine Dietrich Bonhoeffer's book *Life Together* as an example of a Christo-centric ideal of community.[2] Not only does he present the ideal, he also presents in a detailed way a kind of materialism as he describes the way *life together* is lived out: alone, with others, and in active ministry.

MY BELOVED COMMUNITY: OR, THE PLANNING COMMITTEE OF THE JAMES RIVER CHAPTER OF THE VIRGINIA INTERFAITH CENTER FOR PUBLIC POLICY (VICPP)

Or, the Planning Committee of the James River Chapter of the Virginia Interfaith Center for Public Policy (VICPP). Over the course of five months, beginning in March 2020, which coincided with the lockdown in Virginia and in most of the world, John G., Charles, John W., Karen, Walter, Anthony, Betsy, and Christine became *my* beloved community. Together, we were an ethnically diverse group: a nurse, a teacher, one Church of God in Christ pastor, a Baptist pastor, a retired Methodist pastor, a retired pharmaceutical representative, and an unapologetically atheist civil rights activist. By this time, most of the group had known each other and had worked together for more than a year. Yet, we knew very little about our lives outside the

---

2. Bonhoeffer's doctoral dissertation, published later as *Sanctorum Communio,* provide much of the theological and ecclesiological basis of the popular monograph.

group—much less our personal histories. They were unique and very special to me as they were neither family nor, with the exception of one, Lutheran.

A turning point in the group was mid-April when I suggested that we share our personal stories. Not knowing what to expect, I was surprised as one after another shared their personal histories. Career trajectories. Successes and failures. Diverse family of origin stories. Religious pilgrimages. From that point on, the planning group began taking on another dimension. In my mind, subconsciously, I began claiming the group as one of *my* beloved communities.

The symposium "Building the Beloved Community in a Wounded World" took placed on Wednesday, October 7. Attendance was more than we expected. The opening and closing keynotes were excellent and set the stage and provided closure, respectively. The five H presentations were wonderfully diverse, and the number of participants remained steady through the day. The planning group was very pleased, so when the suggestion was made that we have a celebration meeting (via Zoom) an hour and a half after the symposium ended, most the group showed up to review and to celebrate. The mood was ebullient!

Four days later, on a foggy Sunday morning, my wife and I were driving after church to our retirement home on the sunrise side of the Blue Ridge Mountains. We were marking day 210 of our COVID-19 exile, glad to be back worshiping live in a congregation, and basking in the glow of a visit with dear friends after church. The friends were seemingly enraptured by my report of the virtual symposium of which I had been a part. While I related the story of the way the symposium had developed and the positive response it received, what I really emphasized was how the eight-member planning group had become *my* beloved community over the course of the previous five months. Coming down the sunrise side of the Blue Ridge into cell phone coverage, I checked my email messages. Three messages that had arrived within forty-five minutes of each other. Three from *my* beloved community saying that they were done, exhausted, and were leaving the group. Most disturbing was the note from the person who I felt had contributed most to the success of the symposium, indicating a desire to separate immediately from the group. The title of the symposium, "Building the Beloved Community in a Wounded World," suddenly took new meaning. I knew I was wounded and, like soldiers in the field who suffer wounds immediately try to assess the seriousness, I tried to assess what this really meant. My first reaction was to cry out, "Oh no!" Then again after reading the second email, "Oh, no!" And then finally again, "Oh no!" My wife, startled, said, "Philip, what is going on?" With that question the search for meaning began.

Stone's pragmatic frame of the beloved community provides a matrix for understanding *my* beloved community.

- Local. The planning group and the intended audience for the symposium was local. The eight of us lived within a radius of fifteen miles. We represented one of twenty-seven local chapters of the Virginia Interfaith Center for Public Policy. Our advocacy focus continued to be the two congressional districts that we lived in and the senators and members of the House of Delegates that represented us in the Virginia Assembly. Our invite list, provided us by the office of VICPP, included less than four hundred email addresses of those who had contact with VICPP from our zip codes. All of us added additional names, including friends, family, and community contacts. We recruited local agencies, private and nonprofit, to become sponsors of the event. Two of the group were board members of VICPP.

- Voluntary.[3] All of us were volunteers, and most would be considered committed advocates for at least one if not several causes. As I came to know these people, they gave of themselves freely to prophetic action. Two of the group, John W. and Charles, in their commitment to further Medicaid expansion in the state of Virginia, had become aware that the senator who represented their district was the person who prevented the necessary legislation from reaching the floor of the Assembly. For nineteen consecutive weeks, in rain, wind, cold, and even snow, they held vigils in groups of two to ten on the lawn outside his office, with Charles blowing his shofar! When the Medicaid expansion legislation passed, they returned and reseeded the lawn that they had trampled.

- Fallible/Messy. When things are going well and adrenalin is high, it is easy to ignore issues within the group that do not affect you personally but about which you think, "Ouch, that hurts," or, "That was uncalled for." Because the group had argued and worked through so many issues successfully, I think that the rest of the group and I did not pay enough attention to the deeply personal. The group norm included great acceptance of any idea, even the most bizarre being respected, except for two instances that were not processed.

---

3. I am not using this word in Stone's philosophical sense of voluntarism; rather, I am using it simply to mean that in *my* beloved community, none of us were compensated or paid for our roles within the group. Of course, if I were to generalize about beloved communities I would not claim that a beloved community must be comprised *only of* volunteers.

- Experimental. Part of the magical energy of *my* community was the excitement that we were doing something that had not been done before. We had only the previous symposium, which had been totally innovative as a model, and because of the pandemic the playing field for this event was very different. As the planning process went on, the excitement grew as our ideas took shape in action plans. In retrospect, it is the magic of human ingenuity that energizes when the ideal becomes pragmatic.

- Exit Allowed. There was no compulsion to continue to be a part of the group. Members were free to leave.

In addition to Stone's list, I would borrow from Goodson's interpretation of Royce and add three additional characteristics of *my* beloved community.

- A Historical Community of Memory. The first two Hs, heroes and honor, were dependent on memory—those who had stood in the local community for certain issues were profiled and some were interviewed. Deeply moving was the interview of a family that had been devastated by COVID-19. The idea behind these presentations was that the beloved community remembers and honors its heroes by naming them and telling their stories.

- A Community of Expectation or Community of Hope. Our planning group was motivated at least in part by the hope that what we were doing would make a difference in encouraging ourselves and those attending the symposium to work toward making the world a better place. Thinking back, I realize that this motivation was seldom brought to a level of consciousness. All of the presentations reflected the underlying hope that the issues we focused on were critical in building a beloved community in a wounded world. The presentations by Goodson and Stone brought hope front and center, providing a unifying focus, and offering a compelling case for action. The closing keynote challenged all the participants to act.

- Not Systematic but Edifying.[4] Our planning group, primarily because of our leader, John G., was tenacious about the importance of the individual. A group norm was established that early on those who had to be absent would notify the group. We knew who would not be present and in most cases were informed as to why. It seemed that most in

---

4. This characteristic of *my* beloved community comes neither from Goodson nor Stone but serves as my own contribution.

the group were affirmed by their relationships with individuals in the group and with the group as a whole.

So why was I wounded? In therapy, both individual and especially in marriage and family therapy, the lack of differentiation is a primary indicator of intrapersonal and interpersonal dysfunction. Simply stated, differentiation is when there is a firm boundary between where I end and another person or group begins. A helpful term here is emotional enmeshment. Emotional enmeshment takes place when my feelings have been contaminated by a significant other's feelings. I know that I am emotionally enmeshed when I take responsibility for how the others feel. When I am feeling controlled by the other, I know that my differentiation is compromised.

I became emotionally enmeshed with this group. Not that this is necessarily bad; in fact, it is the emotional attachment that at some level is necessary for relationships to survive and thrive. The key is the word "my" in *my* beloved community. As the isolation required by the growing severity of the pandemic, the planning group became a primary place of affirmation as well as a place where I fit in and contributed to something about which I felt very strong. In a sense, the group became *mine* in the same way that—with some legitimacy—we say *my* wife, *my* family, or *my* children.[5] In those situations, we are bound by covenants and by legal responsibility. I am not free to abandon my wife or my children. With the beloved community, especially in extreme cases, the voluntary easily slips into the obligatory—in which I begin to assume responsibility for the other or the group and in which I become entitled to the group's loyalty to me.

Several things at this point become obvious. First is that the planning group was never *my* group. A group as it comes together for whatever reason and around whatever cause is a semi-miracle or, from another perspective, a gift. Second, as our stakes for the success of the symposium grew, we chose to ignore the reality that the group was becoming more than just a group planning an event. We had also become a group that, depending on the emotional and social neediness of the individual members, was important as a community. Not one in the group was new to group experiences: pastors, teachers, salesmen, advocates, nurses—all of these professions depend on competence in being a group member. Naively, we chose to ignore the basic requirements of a functioning group. There are a number of names that describe this necessity: protocols, ground rules, codes of ethics, constitutions, statement of values, mission statements, personnel handbooks, covenants. While everyone was, at one level, certainly aware of the importance

5. For Goodson's reflections on the significance of "mine" and "my," see *Strength of Mind*, xvii.

of the housekeeping work, we as a group chose to act and work as if we did not need to establish the obvious. We had acknowledged the uniqueness of each person in sharing our personal stories, and after the event we gathered to celebrate together its success. But we chose to ignore the inherent vicissitudes of humans working together that protocols, ground rules, etc. attempt to anticipate and provide structure that avoids or repairs the inevitable dysfunction.

THE WASTE HOWLING WILDERNESS: A CASE STUDY

> Without God, this world indeed would be a desert place without an oasis; but thank God, every once in a while, in this waste howling wilderness, we come to a spot what we call, "the Sweet Hour of Prayer." And there this little caravan may stop for a while, and be refreshed with a little talk with Jesus. Let us unload now at that spot and bow our hands and hearts in earnest prayer.[6]

On a sunny afternoon some thirty-five years ago, the "waste howling wilderness" enveloped the "little caravan" known as the Lutheran Church of the Ascension—a congregation I served in Atlanta from 1976 to 1994.[7] Dean Chandler, the only child of a single mother, had fallen off his skateboard in front of his house just blocks from the church and suffered a severe head injury. A passerby summoned aid. Later, my daughters remembered that they had heard sirens. Dean, fifteen, was a classmate of my oldest daughter and had recently been confirmed with her. Claudia, his mother, was notified at work that her son was at the hospital. Dean had recently received his learners' permit, and it was through the information on the permit that she was contacted. Our "little caravan" was devastated.[8] The congregation gathered around Claudia. Earl and Gladys Nolting, an older couple who had "adopted" Claudia and Dean, led the congregation in providing care for Claudia as she kept vigil at the hospital. I made daily visits. We prayed that the hemorrhage in Dean's brain would stop. It did not. Surgery was needed. Then we waited.

During the wait, the community kept vigil. In talking with Claudia thirty-five years later, her memory highlights several aspects of the community. The first was the immediacy of the community's response to her and the way that the response did not falter through weeks of hospitalization. As

---

6. Washington, *Conversations*, 169. This is the preface to a prayer, "Our Need for Thee," attributed to Ralph Mark Gilbert (1899–1956), an African American Baptist preacher.

7. See Washington, *Conversations*, 169.

8. See Washington, *Conversations*, 169.

in situations like this, the shock and the upsetting of life quickly give way to new forms of accommodation so that life goes on. Claudia chose not to leave the hospital. She remembers the difference between the visits of her longtime friends and the visits from her worshiping community. The latter were consistent and significant. Prayer had been a meaningful part of her life since childhood, so the prayers of the community and beyond became an important part of her support. As days stretched into weeks, the prognosis became less optimistic. Doctors prepared her for the probable reality that Dean would never wake up. As she related the story of those weeks, she again and again emphasized the importance of the community—mentioning by name specific acts of kindness, caring, and support. It was not the first time she had been the recipient of the community's care. Two years earlier, she underwent extensive surgery. Commenting on that experience, she said that she thought that she had experienced the worst.

On the fortieth day (yes, the community counted), Dean began to respond and over the course of a couple of weeks he regained consciousness and some mobility. The greatest challenge was speech. Over the next few years, Dean struggled with recovery. Claudia now reports with some pride that Dean is married and lives in Houston where he has been active in AA for the last decade.

This case study is quite different from *my* beloved community. I believe Claudia and Dean's case is similar to situations that have become unremarkable in worshiping communities because beloved communities behave in this way because of who they are.[9] Stone's pragmatic frame for the beloved community—local, voluntary, fallible, experimental, and with an exit option—fits in a different way in an established community where there is a formal organization defined by a specific polity with an established leadership structure, specific rituals for the entire life span, and a theological orientation.[10] People with years of experience in worshiping communities will identify with a specific locality (local).[11]

9. I prefer the term *worshiping community* as it focuses on the people who gather for worship rather than the ambiguous terms of parish, congregation, or church. Even those who have "membership" in a congregation who do not gather will often admit that they are not part of a worshiping community.

10. In this sentence, my use of voluntary returns closer to Stone's philosophical voluntarism. I was a paid clergy member of this community, so I am not using voluntary in this case study the same way I did in the first case study.

11. With the advent of livestreaming worship services, virtual membership became an interesting innovation. Our local congregation had virtual memberships in other states and one from India. Since the pandemic, virtual participation and membership obviously has increased.

In conversations with Claudia for writing this chapter, she never expressed disappointment about how her beloved community responded to her need. She did express disappointment with some of her friends who reached out to her in the immediate aftermath of the accident because they did not follow up with her during the weeks of hospitalization. In my judgment, this disappointment represents Stone's use of fallible for communities.

The "little caravan," which included Dean and his mother, in my memory reached out to her in many different and often creative ways.[12] As the wait continued, many within the community suggested and acted in new ways of support and caring. Occasionally, it was the oases of the "Sweet Hour of Prayer" that provided time for reflection and creativity in supporting Claudia.[13] The community also responded to Dean's peers who were devastated by his injury. Innovation for many communities is the lifeblood and Claudia's "little caravan" excelled in finding ways to support and care.[14] In my judgment, this creativity and innovation represents Stone's use of experimental for communities.

BONHOEFFER'S *LIFE TOGETHER*

In my training as a pastoral psychotherapist and the marriage counseling that my wife and I received, I began to realize that the stridency of the opening chapter of Dietrich Bonhoeffer's *Life Together* found resonance in a widely accepted psychological theory.

Bonhoeffer was born in February 1906 in Breslau, Germany, into a family of seven children, whose parents provided them a rich cultured life of music and literature. His father was a psychiatrist, whose professional life took him in a decidedly different direction than his more famous contemporary, Sigmund Freud. A brilliant student, by the age of sixteen Dietrich knew that he wanted to study theology. By age twenty-one, he presented his first doctoral thesis: a study of the holy Christian church that eventually became the book *Sanctorum Communio*. In a lecture in 1933, he made public his concern about the direction his country was taking in following Hitler. Being broadcast on the radio, Bonhoeffer's lecture was cut off halfway through. Sensing danger, he left for the safe environment of London, where he pastored two worshiping communities. Two years later in 1935, he chose to return to Germany to be the director of an illegal clandestine seminary for the training of young pastors in Pomerania. There, he gathered with

---

12. See Washington, *Conversations*, 169.

13. See Washington, *Conversations*, 169.

14. See Washington, *Conversations*, 169.

a group of twenty-five students to share common life in emergency-built houses. The basic premises of *Sanctorum Communio* would take specific shape as he wrote of his experience as the director of this little seminary.[15] It was already in his doctoral dissertation and the volume that followed shortly, *Act and Being*, that his convictions about the nature of the Christian community became clear: the church is an expression of God's presence in the world in concrete form in the community that gathers around the Word.

The underlying tone of the opening chapter is one of empathy and radical conviction. Empathy is expressed for the Christian who is deprived of "in person" contact with fellow Christians: the home bound, the prisoner, the deployed person. His passionate conviction is expressed in the way he distinguishes between a "human community" based on "the dark, turbid urges and desires of the human mind" and the "community of the Spirit" based on "the clear manifest Word of God in Jesus Christ."[16]

It is difficult not to speculate about the origins of the keen psychological insights that Bonhoeffer shows in his careful analysis of the difference between the spiritual and human communities. His father, Karl Bonhoeffer, was a neurologist/psychiatrist who worked at the Charité—the large university hospital in Berlin—from 1912 to 1938. His father's published work tended more toward the neurological than the psychiatric. I am left only with speculation about the possible influence of the father on his son's insight into the nature of groups. So what was it that gave Bonhoeffer his insights about the human proclivities that lead to human communities becoming toxic? Summarized in the following paragraph, his careful lining out the differences between the ideal "community of Spirit" and the "human community" is a tour de force.

> Perhaps the contrast between spiritual and human reality can be made most clear in the following observation: Within the spiritual community there is never, nor in any way, any "immediate" relationship of one to another, whereas human community expresses a profound, elemental human desire for community, for immediate contact with other human souls, just as in the flesh there is the urge for physical merger with other flesh. Such desire of the human soul seeks a complete fusion of I and Thou, whether this occur in the union of love or, what is after all the same thing, in the forcing of another person into one's sphere of power and influence. Here is where the humanly strong person is in his element, securing for himself the admiration, the love, or the fear of the weak. Here human ties, suggestions, and bonds are everything, and in the immediate community of souls we

15. Bonhoeffer, *Life Together*, 9–11.
16. Bonhoeffer, *Life Together*, 31.

have reflected the distorted image of everything that is originally and solely peculiar to community mediated through Christ.
Thus there is such a thing as human absorption.[17]

The psychological insight that Bonhoeffer in not-so-subtle terms expounds
is the importance of differentiation and the warning of the dangers of human absorption and emotional enmeshment.

Still, my question is where Bonhoeffer found this critical insight. Did
he find it in the example of how Christ in relation to his disciples consistently refused to allow his disciples to be absorbed in his personality? While
Christ certainly was an example in behavior toward those on the margins
and in his compassion for the sick, and while he taught the values of humility and service, it was always at arm's length. Although the disciples did not
get it, it was clear that from the beginning Christ was preparing his disciples
for the time when he would not be with them and the kind of leadership the
community that would arise in his name needed.

Or did this insight come from his own experience? We know that Bonhoeffer's observing ego was quite aware of the magnetism of his persona. He
fought against it. Rather than build a cult around his personality, his writings (e.g., *Letters and Papers from Prison*) and the reports of his relationship with his fiancé, siblings, and fellow prisoners reflect a man intensely
personal—with the intent of being a caring if not a Christ-like presence to
those who came his way.

The ideal is presented in no uncertain terms in the first chapter.[18] The
rest of the book—"The Day with Others"; "The Day Alone"; "Ministry";
and "Confession and Communion"—represent a kind of materialism in the
sense that Bonhoeffer offers specifics that bend toward the autocratic. The
tension will always exist in the implementing of the ideal. In the same way
that the prescriptions for the early Christian community as outlined by Luke
in the Acts of the Apostles and St. Paul in his epistles have been interpreted
in many different ways and implemented in as many ways, so with Bonhoeffer's specifics on the structure of the day alone and the day with others. His
directions may work well in a community of single men who live together
without the responsibility of family or the need to earn a living, but may not
be possible in other living situations. Also, the directions for the spiritual
life with centerpieces being the reading of the Scriptures, confession and
absolution, and receiving holy communion may be appropriate for liturgical
and sacramental Christians, but not for Christians of other traditions. His

17. Bonhoeffer, *Life Together*, 32–33.
18. See Bonhoeffer, *Life Together*, 17–39.

Christocentric beginning point also will be not acceptable to those who are not from the Christian tradition.

An obvious omission of this chapter are case studies from Islamic and Judaic traditions. On this front, research delayed for another time includes the following questions. Are there similar components in all three Abrahamic traditions that contribute to beloved communities? Is one Abrahamic tradition more likely to produce beloved communities than the others? Are there inherent factors in the Abrahamic traditions that result in communities becoming toxic where people are wounded rather than succored? What are those factors? For instance, Bonhoeffer's ideal of beloved community is extraordinarily Christocentric for the exact reason as to protect against the toxic elements that arise in communities. Can there be a beloved community within the Christian tradition without Christ as the center? Do the traditions of Islam and Judaism have a similar essential ingredient, person, or idea that can be identified in their analogous beloved communities so as to prevent toxicity arising within those communities?

SUMMARY CONCLUSION

Case studies by their nature are local, specific, and personal. Case studies and the stories of communities provide a readily available resource for considering the relationship of the ideal to the pragmatic. Immense amounts of data are available to refine the ideal of what community can be. History describes the battlefield and the skeletons of the often-failed efforts to build the beloved community. History also reminds us of the wounded world. Current events make it impossible for us to ignore the continuing wounding of our world. The cacophony of cries is deafening. Arguments will continue about which ideal represents the best hope for building the beloved community.

The first two case studies in this chapter are quite personal. They also represent communities that function well, though imperfectly. Committing to live in community involves both risks and benefits. The first chapter of Bonhoeffer's *Life Together* describes the ideal Christocentric community, the community of Spirit that gets contrasted with a sure-to-fail human community. The remaining chapters in *Life Together* describe in specific ways the material: how the community of Spirit structures its life and calendar.

Careful case studies are the first step toward building beloved community. Avoiding what does not work, expecting messiness, anticipating the fallible, and gleaning what contributes to sustainable beloved communities leave the important work of marrying the ideal with the material. For those intrepid folk who dare, the difficult work of building the beloved community remains.

PART 3

The Current Situation

7

James Baldwin, White "Privilege," and Jouissance

Brad Elliott Stone

ONE KEY PHILOSOPHICAL TASK is the clarification of terms used in knowledge production, testing them for meaning and significance. Although one can appreciate the ways that words, terms, and phrases are used in everyday parlance, their insertion into the order of knowledge can often be fraught with difficulties and presuppositions. It is the philosopher's task to reveal those presuppositions in order to clarify—or, if no such clarification can be made, remove—these words and phrases.

There are many expressions that—although meant to produce what I call *educated well-meaning liberal white people*—are conceptually problematic and in need of philosophical scrutiny. There has been an effort over the past several decades to train (mostly white) students to become more sensitive to the ways in which racism, sexism, heterosexism, ableism, and classism affect people they will encounter in a diverse society. I am not, of course, suggesting that the cultivation of tolerance and the creation of a more inclusive use of language is a bad thing, but I do want to problematize the *whiteness* of such efforts. The goal of such efforts seems to be the creation of what Shannon Sullivan calls "good white people."[1] What would it mean to

1. Cf. Sullivan, *Good White People*.

conceive of a new goal: the elimination of white supremacy, the elimination of the very "whiteness" behind the notions of race, gender, sexuality, class, and ability? I will focus on race here, but the other categories come along with it in, dare I say, the same fashion.

Here is an example. A phrase everyone now knows to say is that "race is a social construction." What such a phrase usually means is that race is not a natural or biological phenomenon. This is true. The Human Genome Project settled the biological debate about races. There is no biological reason we talk about human beings in terms of race. If this is all the phrase "race is a social construction" can mean, I worry that it says too little. Race might be some non-biological natural kind. Early racists offered geographical arguments in lieu of biological ones. Such arguments, however, have also become untenable. Many would claim that race must be a social kind. I am not so sure. After all, there are phenomena that we correctly call "social kinds" (e.g., systems of exchange, governments, languages, and religions), and it seems that race is not like these. So what should be said instead? A more correct thing to say is that "*racism* is a social construction." One can provide a history of racism (Foucault does, for example) and ask the question of why we keep this construction, whether we should dismantle this construction, and what would accelerate that dismantling.

Another term that is used a lot—and will be my focus here—is "privilege." In terms of race and gender theory (among other theories), it is meant to describe the ways in which whiteness and masculinity aid those who "possess" them, establishing and perpetuating inequalities. I seek to challenge this word, not by demonstrating that whiteness and masculinity do not aid white people and men, but by showing that the term (a) fails to account for the real workings of white supremacy and sexism, (b) misunderstands the effects of white supremacy and sexism on those who suffer under it, and (c) is impotent in creating solutions to the problems of white supremacy and sexism. Connected to this word is the more problematic activity of having one "check their privilege," an activity that schools are teaching students to do, including the very people who suffer under white supremacy, sexism, and all other forms of oppression. Worst of all is the word "underprivileged," which suggests that victims of racism, sexism, etc., are simply unlucky and were dealt a bad hand, which simply is not the case. Black people, for example, do not consider themselves unlucky or "underprivileged." They find themselves *under attack, under surveillance*, sometimes wrongfully *under arrest*, etc. These are the direct result of white supremacy, not chance. In short, one cannot capture the experiences of "non-privileged" people in terms of the alleged "benefits" of "privilege."

In fact, it is this very language of "benefits" and "advantage" that makes talk of privilege problematic. Instead of wondering how one benefits from whiteness, masculinity, etc., one could wonder why one considers whiteness, masculinity, etc., to be *beneficial*. Beneficial for what? If they are only beneficial for life in a racist, sexist, etc., state, wouldn't I want to bring an end to such a state instead of simply to gain the benefits thereof? It also suggests that—even in a racist, sexist, etc., state—nonwhites and nonmales would have benefits of some kind. After all, is there something about me being a Black man that either (a) keeps me from alleged benefits or (b) causes me to be somehow *impeded* by virtue of my Blackness? Is it really the case that my alleged "male privilege" allows me to "overcome" my alleged "Black underprivilege"? What if I had neither male privilege nor Black underprivilege? Intersectionality intensifies the criticism, as privilege talk has to balance all the different elements in ways that assumes that this-trumps-that and that there is a "race to the bottom" in which multiple forms of oppression overlapping each other create increased oppression, disadvantage, and thus critical power.

At the heart of the discussion of "privilege" is a presupposition that there is something good or beneficial about being white, male, etc. I respond that there is no reason to hold that presupposition. James Baldwin is probably the most unambiguous writer on this point. Baldwin's racial antirealism concerning white people resists any true positive claim about white advantage in a racist world. Whether one counts Baldwin among the philosophers is its own debate, but his literary nonfiction offers sufficient conceptual analysis, phenomenological description, and existential hermeneutics to be of philosophical use.

Finding the right word to replace "privilege" is tricky, but I propose a word: *jouissance*. It is a word found throughout French philosophy and psychoanalysis. I will focus today on Levinas's sense of the term found in *Totality and Infinity*. One philosophical advantage of describing white privilege as white *jouissance* is that Levinas provides us with the solution to that *jouissance* in terms of responsibility, which fully expresses itself in terms of what he calls "substitution" in *Otherwise than Being*. Baldwin also presents a notion of substitution in response to the weight and burden of whiteness.

This essay proceeds in three parts. In the first part, I explicate Levinas's ethical phenomenology in order to highlight the movement from *jouissance* to substitution. This is the theoretical lens I will use to frame the chapter. I then turn to Baldwin's antirealism and his critique of white *jouissance*. At the heart of that critique will be his antirealism about whiteness and his views on white ignorance. In the third part of the essay, I will outline white privilege in terms of white *jouissance* and propose how Black people serve as Levinasian Others as well as Levinasian moral agents in their own right (both at the same time).

LEVINAS ON AUTONOMY, JOUISSANCE, AND RESPONSIBILITY

Levinas's description of autonomy in the 1957 "Philosophy and the Idea of Infinity" differs from the traditional political definition in terms of self-rule: "Autonomy, the philosophy which aims to ensure the freedom, or the identity, of beings, presupposes that freedom itself is sure of its right, is justified without recourse to anything further, is complacent in itself, like Narcissus."[2] Notice that autonomy for Levinas is not self-rule, but a philosophical assumption that freedom is foundationally basic. In Levinas's works, freedom is presented in terms of identity, spontaneity, *pouvoir* (my ability to do something, my ability to "can do"), arbitrariness, narcissism, and violence. No surprise, then, that violence is often the result of the clashes between two different identities, freedoms, powers, etc.

The answer to this freedom, this autonomy, is the Other. The Other is the one who "is exposed to all my powers, succumbs to all my rules, all my crimes. Or he resists me with all his force and all the unpredictable resources of his own freedom. I measure myself against him."[3] This notion of the Other makes it seem as if the Other is some other, equally autonomous force against which one would have to assert one's own identity. But Levinas reverses our expectations, stating that the Other "does not stop me like a force blocking my force; it puts into question the naïve right of my powers, my glorious spontaneity."[4] Thus Levinas's Other is not like Hegel's master-slave dialectic nor Sartre's gaze; it is not a battle to the death between two autonomous agents. Rather, one's own freedom is put into question and shown to be naïve. As Levinas describes it, "*I am no longer able to have power*: the structure of my freedom is . . . completely reversed."[5] This does not mean that one becomes controlled by the Other or unable to "can"; rather, what is reversed is the claim of freedom that accompanies such actions: "Freedom is put into question by the other, and is revealed to be unjustified, only when it knows itself to be unjust. Its knowing itself to be unjust is not something added on to spontaneous and free consciousness, which would be present

---

2. Levinas, "Philosophy and the Idea of Infinity," 49.
3. Levinas, "Philosophy and the Idea of Infinity," 55.
4. Levinas, "Philosophy and the Idea of Infinity," 58.
5. Levinas, "Philosophy and the Idea of Infinity," 55.

to itself and know itself to be, *in addition*, guilty."[6] This guilt is at the very root of the autonomous demand for freedom in the presence of the Other. Before the Other, my assertion of self-identity becomes itself an injustice and a cause for shame: "It is a *shame* freedom has of itself, discovering itself to be murderous and usurpatory in its very exercise."[7] For Levinas, there is no neutral use of one's freedom; freedom always has a cost that is somehow paid by the Other. One's autonomy is grounded in heteronomy.

The task of the Levinasian project, as stated in *Totality and Infinity*, is to begin "in discourse a non-allergic relation with alterity" since "I cannot disentangle myself from society with the Other."[8] *Totality and Infinity* offers a phenomenological account of this inability to be truly autonomous. This inability is defined in terms of an asymmetry: "the radical impossibility of seeing oneself from the outside and of speaking in the same sense of oneself and of the others . . . and, on the plane of social experience, the impossibility of *forgetting* the intersubjective experience that leads to that social experience and endows it with meaning."[9] In other words, contrary to the Husserlian project of egological intersubjectivity, where one language can speak for both oneself and another (as simply another "I" in the life-world), Levinas points to the insufficiency of one's own language to adequately *capture* the Other. The Other speaks to me, and in so doing does not speak my language but a different one. As a result, I cannot ignore that I am in the presence of something other than myself.

When the Other is not speaking to me, I might *forget* that my existence is dependent upon the Other. Levinas describes this as "separation" or "enjoyment" (*jouissance*).[10] Levinas describes enjoyment as follows: "In enjoyment I am absolutely for myself. Egoist without reference to the Other, I am alone . . . innocently egoist and alone. Not against the Others . . . but entirely deaf to the Other, outside of all communication and all refusal to communicate."[11] Since the Other *speaks* to me, enjoyment is a kind of deafness that need not hearken the Other or strain too hard to hear the call of the Other. Rather, one could innocently consider themselves alone in the world—self-creating and self-causing.

6. Levinas, "Philosophy and the Idea of Infinity," 50–51.

7. Levinas, "Philosophy and the Idea of Infinity," 58.

8. Levinas, *Totality and Infinity*, 47.

9. Levinas, *Totality and Infinity*, 53.

10. The term *jouissance* has several meanings in French, but here "enjoyment" simply means a life defined in one's own terms, the illusory realm of autonomy.

11. Levinas, *Totality and Infinity*, 134.

But even enjoyment is not completely free from having to consider alterity. Levinas notes that alterity enters even the real of enjoyment, not through other people, but through inconveniences that threaten comfort and produce feelings of insecurity. One such thing is the future itself: unknown, uncontrollable, unpredictable. Thus even within enjoyment there is something outside of oneself, something with which one may or may not have to deal.

Levinas explains this in more detail in *Existence and Existents*. The alleged autonomous life is unsatisfactory, unsatisfying, and unenjoyable due to its resistance to the true reality of alterity. Hoarding Being for itself, *jouissance* results in anxiety, indolence, and fatigue. Since *jouissance* is actually a make-believe of autonomy, there is an anxiety concerning how long one has for play. If one is truly autonomous, it would be up to the autonomous one to make the future what it is going to be. Yet, since the future is unknown, uncontrollable, and unpredictable, autonomy faces anxiety for the future. Indolence, or laziness, is for Levinas about the impossibility of beginning. Just as anxiety means that one does not know how the future is going to be, *jouissance* never does history. The past means nothing to the autonomous; there cannot be a "beginning." The autonomous one never gets around to establishing the conditions of the present. Between past and future, between anxiety and indolence, is fatigue. Since autonomy presupposes that it is alone and the sole agent of action, *jouissance* wears one out. Dare we say that too much enjoyment is exhausting.

Fleeing from a past and fearing a future, and too worn out in the present, *jouissance* is best understood from the point of view of *Existence and Existents* as an *evasion*. Autonomy is actually not the primary form of subjectivity; it is an effort to escape a world that is actually filled with other people. By fleeing the responsibility owed to others, one becomes responsible for ironically much more. It is indeed harder to live alone than with others. *Jouissance*, in the end, is no fun.

In contrast, "[t]he presence of the Other is equivalent to this calling into question of my joyous possession of the world."[12] The world is a shared one, and the Other appears as proof of that fact. Thus one's autonomy now appears as violence. The Other "is *ipso facto* the consciousness of my own injustice—the shame that freedom proves about itself."[13] Levinas calls this phenomenon of the Other the face (*visage*). Before the face of the Other, I can do one of two things: (1) learn from the other the violence of my sense of autonomy, or (2) "kill" the Other by disregarding the moral imperative it

12. Levinas, *Totality and Infinity*, 75–76.
13. Levinas, *Totality and Infinity*, 86; translation amended.

speaks. The face's commandment, "Thou shalt not kill," is not a prohibition of murder *per se* but rather the request to not turn the Other into some kind of extension of one's self. In other words, the face commands, "*Thou shalt not kill off the reality of alterity from your consciousness.*" In fact, murder *per se* is only a secondary act; the first murder already happened in order to consider the life of the other person as expendable, as something in one's world of enjoyment and possession. All moral offenses work similarly.

Thus, in the presence of the demand of the Other, I realize that I am responsible for what I do, that I must answer for what I do. In enjoyment I am care-less about responding to the Other about my activities, but when the face appears, I am called to account. This call is not a violence done upon me; rather, it is an invitation for me to consider violence. Violence would be the negative response to the call; responsibility would be the positive response. Thus, for Levinas, my possibilities before the Other—responsibility or violence—serve as the condition of the possibility of any ethical system or even oneself as a subject at all. As Levinas notes in *Otherwise than Being*, "[r]esponsibility for another is not an accident that happens to a subject . . . The ipseity . . . is a hostage. The word *I* means *here I am*, answering for everything and for everyone."[14] Before the Other, one must answer, either with *here I am* (responsibility) or *you are not* (murder).

This responsibility, Levinas tells us, is asymmetrical. In an interview with Philippe Nemo in *Ethics and Infinity*, Levinas states that "I am responsible for the Other without waiting for reciprocity, were I to die for it. Reciprocity is *his* [the Other's] affair."[15] One alone is responsible, whether or not the Other is. Levinas talks about responsibility in terms of being responsible to everyone for everything. If one wants autonomy, one must be responsible for all things. What might be more telling is that one often seeks to shunt responsibility to someone else while nonetheless claiming autonomy, which is a performative contradiction.

Being responsible for everything and for everyone is what Levinas calls substitution. One is required by alterity to substitute for those who have done wrong and have been wronged. This substitution is itself asymmetrical: "I can substitute myself for everyone, but no one can substitute himself for me . . . It is in this precise sense that Dostoevsky said: "*We are all responsible for all, for all men before all, and I more than all the others.*"[16]

14. Levinas, *Otherwise than Being*, 114.
15. Levinas, *Ethics and Infinity*, 98.
16. Dostoevsky, *The Brothers Karamazov,* quoted in Levinas, *Ethics and Infinity*, 101.

BALDWIN ON ANTIREALISM AND
WHITE IGNORANCE

In this section, I turn to James Baldwin's writings. As Cornel West notes in *Democracy Matters*, "Baldwin spoke from the position of the oppressed 'other' in our culture."[17] This is true, but what makes Baldwin interesting to me is that he also requires that white people be seen as the Black's Other, and that Black people—like it or not—are responsible for whites. As we will see in the next section, this movement from oppressed other to substitution for the Other is a key point of interest when reading Baldwin in light of Levinas.

Throughout the rest of this chapter, Baldwin will be quoted in a series of block quotes, allowing us to enjoy his wording. Reading Baldwin as a philosopher is tricky since he did not write in a philosophical style. Instead, there are moments of insight that appear within his prose. John Drabinski says it best when he writes that "[o]ne of the quirky features of Baldwin's intellectual legacy is our tendency to render this thought in quips and sound bites. There is, it seems, a Baldwin quote for every moment."[18] Like Pascal's sentences or Nietzsche's aphorisms, one has to simply assemble Baldwin passages that collectively can serve as some kind of argumentative support for the claim that Baldwin held a particular philosophical position. I do this here.

Baldwin's Antirealism

"[A]ll of the American categories of male and female, straight or not, black or white, were shattered, thank heaven, very early in my life."[19] Baldwin, a gay Black writer, although front and center in both the civil rights and gay rights movements, finds identity politics too constricting and binding. Throughout Baldwin's corpus, we find an antirealism that truly liberates. This antirealism, ironically, is grounded in a realism about everything else: the nature of vulnerability and suffering, the cold silence of the world, and an atheism from which Baldwin could nonetheless preach and evangelize. Baldwin mostly points his antirealism towards white people, insisting throughout his writings that white people are not real. White people,

17. West, *Democracy Matters*, 79.

18. Drabinski, "James Baldwin," 481.

19. Baldwin, "Freaks and the American Ideal of Manhood," 819. Unless otherwise noted, references to all Baldwin essays, including passages from *The Fire Next Time*, are from this anthology.

Baldwin claims over and over again, "are not really white."[20] There is no natural reality in which white people are white. Similarly, of course, there is no natural reality in which nonwhite people are nonwhite. Baldwin tells us this in three passages:

> Color is not a human or a personal reality; it is a political reality.[21]

> It does not seem to me that nature helps us very much when we need illumination in human affairs.[22]

> [W]hite men believe the world is theirs and . . . expect the world to help them in the achievement of their identity. But the world does not do this—for anyone.[23]

Race, Baldwin contends, is a political reality—a by-product of the social construction of racist society. There is no natural reality expressed by the concept of race. Whatever ultimate reality is, it does not entail the invention of whiteness and the subsequent creation of racist politics. This is all strictly a historical, political, and thus a human affair.

At the heart of Baldwin's analysis of whiteness is that whiteness is a lie that attempts to get around the existence of Black people. Whiteness is the wish to avoid the encounter with Black people, to go back to a time when Black people didn't insist on their lives mattering. Against this dream, Baldwin responds with the harsh reality of not only Black existence, but the fact that this Black existence has been here all along. America, Baldwin reminds over and over throughout his writings, starts multiracially from the very first moment. Not only were there first nations present on the land, but Black people came alongside the European settlers. There is no story of America that does not involve Black people. This, Baldwin argues, is why white Americans pine over Europe: Black people did not exist there. Such pining, of course, makes no sense. America has never been white in that European sense (and, it is worth pointing out, Europe itself is no longer that magic white haven imagined by white Americans).

> [I]n effect, the black man, *as a man*, did not exist for Europe. But in America, even as a slave, he was an inescapable part of the general social fabric and no American could escape having an attitude toward him.[24]

20. Baldwin, "Color," 673.
21. Baldwin, *The Fire Next Time*, 345–46.
22. Baldwin, "The Male Prison," 232.
23. Baldwin, "The Black Boy Looks at the White Boy," 279.
24. Baldwin, "Stranger in the Village," 125.

American white men still nourish the illusion that there is some means of recovering the European innocence, of returning to a state in which black men do not exist. This is one of the greatest errors Americans can make.[25]

Europe has never been, and cannot be, a useful or valid touchstone for the American experience because America is not, and never can be, white.[26]

The European image of the black man rests finally, one must say, on [proper] ignorance, and, however expedient this ignorance may be, it is sustained by the objective conditions [of there not being black people around]; whereas the American image of the Negro has been created . . . and is sustained by an anguished inability to come to terms . . . This heritage deprives us entirely of the kind of racial innocence which one finds in Europe.[27]

Baldwin never finds the Europeans' fascination with his skin color problematic (although he does find it annoying). He is fine being the stranger in some Swiss village or an American in Paris. The problem is that in New York City, in the United States, he is supposed to be a stranger of the same kind. That makes no sense given the history of this country.

The other side of white supremacy includes the hope of an all-white future (even if one cannot return to an "all-white" past). This too is impossible. Baldwin ends "Stranger in the Village" with a stark reminder: "The world is white no longer, and it will never be white again."[28] The dream of whiteness, "the price of the ticket," as Baldwin would say, is built on an impossibility.[29] Instead there is only that thing that white people call "the Negro problem" (and, taking a dig at DuBois, Baldwin reminds us that "there is no such thing as a Negro problem").[30] What is this problem? The presence of Black people shatters the illusion of an exclusive whiteness.

[T]he price of the ticket is involved—fatally—with the dream of becoming white. This is not possible, partly because white

---

25. Baldwin, "Stranger in the Village," 128.
26. Baldwin, "The Price of the Ticket," 836.
27. Baldwin, "The Negro at Home and Abroad," 604.
28. Baldwin, "Stranger in the Village," 129.
29. Baldwin, "The Price of the Ticket," 835.
30. Baldwin, "Words of a Native Son," 713.

people are not white: part of the price of the ticket is to delude themselves into believing that they are.[31]

At the root of the American Negro problem is the necessity of the American white man to find a way of living with the Negro in order to be able to live with himself.[32]

White Ignorance

Baldwin's *The Fire Next Time* offers an account both of ignorance and of ignoring. These are not equi-primordial for Baldwin: ignorance is the result of ignoring. In "My Dungeon Shook," an open letter written to his nephew who is also named James, Baldwin tells James that as far as white people are concerned, "most of them do not yet really know that you exist."[33] Baldwin continues by saying that James's existence is known by Baldwin and Baldwin's mother, although "[y]our countrymen don't know that *she* exists, either, though she has been working for them all their lives."[34] Baldwin repeats this motif in "Down at the Cross," an essay he wrote for *The New Yorker* that makes up the majority of *The Fire Next Time*: "I am proud of [black people] not because of their color but because of their intelligence and their spiritual force and their beauty. The country should be proud of them, too, but, alas, not many people in this country even know of their existence."[35]

The existence of Black people in America is one of invisibility, as Ralph Ellison so wonderfully shows in *Invisible Man*. Of course, that there are Black people is plain to see; the invisibility has to do with the role that Blacks can play. As Baldwin tells James,

> You were born where you were born and faced the future that you faced because you were black and *for no other reason*. The limits of your ambition were, thus, expected to be set forever. You were born into a society which spelled out with brutal clarity, and in as many ways as possible, that you were a worthless human being.[36]

31. Baldwin, "The Price of the Ticket," 835.
32. Baldwin, "Stranger in the Village," 127.
33. Baldwin, *The Fire Next Time*, 292.
34. Baldwin, *The Fire Next Time*, 292.
35. Baldwin, *The Fire Next Time*, 344.
36. Baldwin, *The Fire Next Time*, 293.

As long as Blacks fulfill the role of the worthless human being, all is well. However, it is when Blacks become visible that crisis emerges, or when the Black experience is used outside of its pre-established confines.

This ignoring of Blacks produces what Charles Mills calls *white ignorance*. This ignorance, Mills tells us, is above and beyond—frankly, it is *contrary to*—epistemological questions concerning knowledge and ignorance. For Baldwin, white ignorance works on several levels. First, whites do not know enough about Blacks in proportion to what Blacks know about whites. As Baldwin writes, "Negroes know far more about white Americans . . . it can almost be said, in fact, that they know about white Americans what parents . . . know about their children."[37] Stated differently further on, Baldwin presents his claim as a direct challenge: "Ask any Negro what he knows about white people with whom he works. And then ask the white people with whom he works what they know about *him*."[38] So the first level of white ignorance has to do with simply not knowing enough about Black people and their experiences. Similarly, Blacks know about whites things that surprise whites. Referring to the Holocaust, Baldwin writes that "white people were astounded by the Holocaust in Germany. They did not know that they could act that way. But I very much doubt whether Black people were astounded—at least, in the same way."[39]

The greater level of ignorance takes the form of a white parochialism which limits what and how whites can come to understand Blacks. In *The Evidence of Things Not Seen*, Baldwin writes that "White Americans . . . are quite unable to imagine that there can be anyone, anywhere, who does not wish to be White."[40] This is the heart of Baldwin's critique of integration. Integration simply moved Blacks into white schools and provided Blacks access to white institutions. The inverse did not happen, which strengthened the idea that whites are at a higher level than Blacks, and that Blacks were fighting for the opportunity to "move up" to that level. Baldwin accuses whites of not seeing that integration might be an invitation for whites to "move up" to the level of Blacks.

The tragedy of such ignorance is that it produces a self-ignorance. White ignorance is not simply an ignorance about Blacks—it makes themselves invisible, too, and this has real ramifications. Baldwin states that

---

37. Baldwin, *The Fire Next Time*, 344.

38. Baldwin, *The Fire Next Time*, 345.

39. Baldwin, *The Fire Next Time*, 317. The same can be said about the 2016 election of Donald Trump.

40. Baldwin, *The Evidence of Things Not Seen*, 23.

white people are "still trapped in a history which they do not understand."[41] By wanting to ignore the ignoring and the ignorance produced by such ignoring, whites fail to face their own legacy of white supremacy. In *The Evidence of Things Not Seen*, Baldwin claims that white ignorance leads to an ignorance about whiteness: "Most White North Americans are always lying to, and concerning, their darker brother, which means that they are always lying to themselves."[42] White ignorance becomes white not-wanting-to-know-to-tell-the-truth. Baldwin tells James that white people "have destroyed and are destroying hundreds of thousands of lives and do not know it and do not want to know it."[43] White ignorance involves not only a lack of knowing, but a decision, a decision not-to-know.

It is the decision to not want to know that moves Baldwin to the moral level. He writes that "it is not permissible that the authors of devastation should also be innocent. It is the innocence which constitutes the crime."[44] White innocence and, as Shelby Steele has shown so wonderfully, white guilt avoid the true moral call that Baldwin wishes to make. White ignorance involves the belief that somehow the problems that face Black America have nothing to do with them; they are puzzled that Blacks continue to be angry with the state of things. We must see that this innocence is itself part of the ignorance, making white ignorance itself morally questionable. Baldwin makes two interesting claims about white innocence and white guilt.

The first is that white ignorance produces a kind of *akrasia* or weakness of will so that whites who have "wised up" are still unable to do anything. Baldwin writes, "[I]t is clear that white Americans are not simply unwilling to effect these changes; they are, in the main, so slothful have they become, unable even to envision them."[45] Stated more directly in the letter to James, Baldwin states that whites "had to believe for many years, and for innumerable reasons, that Black men are inferior to white men. Many of them, indeed, know better, but . . . people find it very difficult to act on what they know."[46] The moral outrage to white innocence is that, to use a well-known phrase, "they know better than that." Unfortunately, contrary to the Black form of that idiom, for 1960s white people, their mamas didn't teach them better than that.

41. Baldwin, *The Fire Next Time*, 294.
42. Baldwin, *The Evidence of Things Not Seen*, 43.
43. Baldwin, *The Fire Next Time*, 292.
44. Baldwin, *The Fire Next Time*, 292.
45. Baldwin, *The Fire Next Time*, 335.
46. Baldwin, *The Fire Next Time*, 294.

The second has to do with white guilt, which allows whites to distance themselves from action by simply taking up a kind of feeling. This, Baldwin argues, prohibits a full relationship with Blacks. His criticism of white liberals is that they "could easily deal with the Negro as a symbol or a victim but had no sense of him as a man."[47] By turning Black people into charity cases, whites could "do something for the Blacks" without having to put themselves into question. The movement from charity to justice, after all, is the acknowledgment that we might be responsible for the very problem that leads to one needing our charity.

Baldwin's solution to the problem of ignorance and innocence is love. This love is not a mere warm feeling, but a persistent, almost Socratic, forcing of whites to examine themselves. Baldwin tells James that "we, with love, shall force our brothers to see themselves as they are, to cease fleeing from reality and begin to change it."[48] In fact, Baldwin proposes that white innocence is simply this flight from reality: "[W]hat we call the Negro problem is produced by the white man's profound desire not to be judged by those who are not white, not to be seen as he is."[49] The end of white ignorance will come by forcing, with love, white people to pay attention to the witness of the Black experience. This end of white ignorance will not only free Blacks, it will free white people from their own self-inflicted self-deception.

BLACK RESPONSIBILITY AND SUBSTITUTION IN RESPONSE TO WHITE PRIVILEGE

Black people cannot afford to be deceived. As Baldwin states, "[I]f I didn't know how power worked, I would be dead . . . I have simply never been able to afford myself any illusions."[50] White privilege might simply be the ability to deceive oneself, which, qua self-deception, would not be considered a benefit or good. Deception is indeed powerful, as Baldwin points out: "[T]here are too many things we do not wish to know about ourselves."[51] Black people, however, have had to embody a reality that is unavoidable and ontologically obvious: "[W]hat white Americans do not face when they regard a Negro: reality—the fact that life is tragic. Life is tragic simply because the earth turns . . . the fact of death, which is the only fact we have."[52] White

---

47. Baldwin, *The Fire Next Time*, 320.
48. Baldwin, *The Fire Next Time*, 294.
49. Baldwin, *The Fire Next Time*, 341.
50. Baldwin, "The Black Boy Looks at the White Boy," 279.
51. Baldwin, *The Fire Next Time*, 337.
52. Baldwin, *The Fire Next Time*, 339.

people's obsession with race might simply be evasion from reality; racism is a system of *jouissance*. But there is a price for *jouissance*: anxiety, indolence, and fatigue.

Yet, all of this white *jouissance* takes place in a world with nonwhite people who often serve as the material and cultural condition for the very possibility of something like a white identity. This is why the effort of "checking one's white privilege" is ironically the entrenchment of that very privilege. There is no autonomous solution to the anxiety, indolence, and fatigue of the autonomous life.

What should happen instead? Responsibility to the other, the recognition that reality weighs upon us in ways that are not our ways, the move from autonomy to heteronomy through substitution. In fact, Baldwin's solution to the agony that white people feel under a racist regime is to become Black. By this, Baldwin is not suggesting that one should change their skin color or give up one's own way of being. Rather, Baldwin is demanding that, like Black people have demonstrated for almost four hundred years in the US, white people face the realities of their situation and open themselves to what Unamuno calls the "tragic sense of life."[53] In doing so, we will realize that we are all human, all facing the same problems, and able to live meaningful lives together.

> The only way [the white man] can be released from the Negro's tyrannical power over him is to consent, in effect, to become black himself, to become a part of that suffering and dancing country that he now watches wistfully from the heights of his lonely power.[54]

> I'm not interested in anybody's guilt. Guilt is a luxury that we can no longer afford. I know you didn't do it, and I didn't do it either, but I am responsible for it because I am a man and a citizen of this country and you are responsible for it, too, for the very same reason.[55]

> [T]he Negro is *not* happy in his place, and white people aren't happy in their place, either.[56]

---

53. See Unamano, *Tragic Sense of Life*.
54. Baldwin, *The Fire Next Time*, 341.
55. Baldwin, "Words of a Native Son," 713.
56. Baldwin, "Color," 674.

All racist positions baffle and appall me. None of us are that different from one another, neither that much better nor that much worse.[57]

We cannot be free until they are free.[58]

Responsibility and substitution means that we realize that we all face the same existential crisis. We are actually all on the same journey through this thing called life. Privilege language exaggerates difference for the sake of identity. Movement to the Other minimizes those distances, creating a *proximity* (to use Levinas's term) that has always already been the case. We all bear the enormous weight of history, and our different stories are simply movements within one story. If white privilege has any innocent meaning, it means that white people play their line of the score without noticing the symphony.

57. Baldwin, "Negroes Are Anti-Semitic Because They Are Anti-White," 747.
58. Baldwin, *The Fire Next Time*, 295.

8

Hatred and Hell yet Hopefulness

Jacob L. Goodson

I . . . found white people to be unutterably menacing, terrifying, mysterious—
wicked: the unfathomable question being . . . this one: what, under heaven, or
beneath the sea, or in the catacombs of hell, could cause any people to act as
white people acted?[1]

INTRODUCTION

Brad Elliott Stone seeks to replace the term "white privilege" with the French
philosophical notion of *jouissance*. His reasons against the term "white privilege" are the following: (a) the term "white privilege" automatically suggests
that non-whites are "underprivileged," but privilege is not what's at issue in
racism (hatred, violence, etc., represent the problems of racism); (b) talking
about racism in terms of privilege makes racism a problem of chance, not
choice (racism is "the direct result of white supremacy, not chance"[2]); and
(c) "At the heart of the discussion of 'privilege' is a presupposition that there

---

1. Baldwin, *The Devil Finds Work*, 481.
2. Stone above, 108.

is something good or beneficial about being white, male, etc. I respond that there is no reason to hold that presupposition."[3]

According to Stone, the French notion of *jouissance* captures how racism functions in American society. Referencing the French Jewish philosopher Emmanuel Levinas, Stone offers readers an especially clear paragraph on what he means.

> When the Other is not speaking to me, I might "forget" that my existence is depending on the Other. Levinas describes this as "separation" or "enjoyment" (*jouissance*). Levinas describes enjoyment as follows: "In enjoyment I am absolutely for myself. Egoist without reference to the Other . . . Not against the Others . . . but entirely deaf to the Other, outside of all communication and all refusal to communicate." Since the Other *speaks* to me, enjoyment is a kind of deafness that need not hearken the Other or strain too hard to hear the call of the Other. Rather, one could innocently consider themselves alone in the world . . .[4]

Using this as a framework for understanding racism, white people in the US think of their lives in terms of the kind of autonomy critiqued by Levinas: an autonomy best understood as *jouissance*—a separation from others. This kind of autonomy is illusory as one's existence does not take place in a vacuum, even in a vacuum that contains only other white people. What makes someone a racist is to think that one can enjoy their lives without encountering or engaging with those who look different from them, so one who is racist develops a kind of *deafness* to the existence of those who look different.

Stone argues that *jouissance* leads to three problems for someone who is racist. *Jouissance* makes a person who is racist anxious, indolent, and fatigued. Stone writes, "*Jouissance* results in anxiety, indolence, and fatigue. Since *jouissance* is actually a make-believe of autonomy, there is an anxiety concerning how long one has for play."[5] Stone's use of the word indolent seems to mean both apathetic and lazy: apathetic in the sense that one does not want to know the history or stories of others, and lazy in the sense that one does not want to know one's own real or true family history. Concerning fatigue, Stone writes: "Since autonomy presupposes that it is alone and the sole agent of action, *jouissance* wears one out. Dare we say that too much enjoyment is exhausting."[6] Although those who are racist think their lives

3. Stone above, 109.
4. Stone above, 111.
5. Stone above, 112.
6. Stone above, 112.

are more enjoyable without encountering or engaging with those who look different from them, in the end *"Jouissance . . .* is no fun."[7]

In this chapter, I continue the conversation started by Stone in the previous chapter. First, I build from the previous paragraph on anxiety, indolence, and fatigue, and connect Stone's use of past, present, and future for understanding racism to arguments I made in chapter 4 concerning how the past and future determine beloved community. Second, still following Stone, I argue that Baldwin's notion of white ignorance ought to replace the term white privilege when talking about and thinking through the problems of racism. This is when I introduce and work through the metaphor of hell for diagnosing racism in the US. Third, I address the problem of white resentment from the angle of Immanuel Kant's Enlightenment philosophy. I conclude with autobiographical reflections on the most intense manifestation of racism and white supremacy experienced and witnessed in my own life.

The thesis for this chapter involves multiple claims. Instead of building beloved community, racism does all that it can to prevent and tear down communities: I defend this claim by examining the role of past, present, and future for both beloved communities and racist communities. Racism creates a hellish society for all persons. According to Baldwin, the difference only concerns one of knowledge vs. ignorance: Black people tend to know they inhabit hell whereas white people remain ignorant of the hell that they have created. Finally, white ignorance and white resentment resemble what Immanuel Kant calls "immaturity" in his famous essay, "What Is Enlightenment?"[8]

PAST, PRESENT, AND FUTURE IN BELOVED COMMUNITIES VS. RACIST COMMUNITIES

Josiah Royce connects what he means by beloved community with philosophical notions of past and future. As I argue in chapter 4,

> the beloved community is one which has a truthful memory of the past and a hopeful expectation of the future. The beloved community is a community of truthful memory in the sense that it is, in the words of Royce, a "community constituted by the fact that each of its members accepts as part of his own individual life . . . the same past events that each of his fellow-members accepts, may be called a *community of memory.*" To be a community of memory means: (a) avoiding using history to

7. Stone above, 112.

8. See Kant, "What Is Enlightenment?," para. 2.

justify our own self-interests, (b) being truthful about history even when doing so makes us feel uncomfortable about ourselves or our family, and (c) identifying the wounds of the past.

Beloved community is also a community of hopeful expectation. In Royce's words, a "community constituted by the fact that each of its members accepts, as part of his own individual life . . . , the same expected future events that each of his fellows accepts, may be called a *community of expectation*, or . . . a *community of hope*." To be a community of hope means: (a) being orientated toward the future—more specifically, toward actualizing the beloved community, (b) being truthful about the past because beloved community cannot be achieved if there is a refusal concerning truthfulness about the past, and (c) thinking of beloved community as the achievement and embodiment of faith, hope, and love.[9]

Now, let's contrast this with Stone's argument concerning how *jouissance* can be understood in terms of past, present, and future.

If one is truly autonomous, it would be up to the autonomous one to make the future what it is going to be. Yet, since the future is unknown, uncontrollable, and unpredictable, autonomy faces *anxiety for the future*. Indolence, or laziness, is for Levinas about the impossibility of beginning. Just as *anxiety means that one does not how the future is going to be, jouissance never does history*. The past means nothing to the autonomous; there cannot be a "beginning." The autonomous one never gets around to establishing the conditions of the present. Between past and future, between anxiety and indolence, is fatigue. Since autonomy presupposes that it is alone and the sole agent of action, *jouissance* wears one out. Dare we say that too much enjoyment is exhausting.

Fleeing from a past and fearing a future, and too worn out in the present, jouissance is best understood . . . as an *evasion*. Autonomy is actually not the primary form of subjectivity; it is an effort to escape a world that is actually filled with other people.[10]

A beloved community requires hard work, honesty, and truthfulness about rehearsing and understanding the past—even, perhaps especially, one's own past in terms of one's own family history; a racist community neither wants to know the history or stories of others (apathy), nor to do the hard work of telling the truth about their own family history (laziness). A beloved

---

9. Goodson above, 72.

10. Stone above, 112; emphasis added.

community seeks for the future to be determined by faith, hope, and love; a racist community displays only anxiety and fearfulness about the future because they are afraid the so-called gains of others automatically means a loss for themselves. Building beloved community requires truthtelling about the past and hopeful expectations about the future in regards to faith, hope, and love being the dominant characteristics of particular communities; racist communities attempt to prevent the building of such communities by whitewashing the past and making the future seem hopeless because of the loss of *jouissance*. Instead of building beloved community, racism and white supremacy do all they can to prevent and tear down communities—the communities of others and their own communities because they refuse to tell the truth about themselves and their history.

THE METAPHOR OF HELL AND THE PROBLEMS OF WHITE IGNORANCE AND WHITE RESENTMENT

The transition between the former section and this section involves another insight from Stone's previous chapter. Stone claims, "The other side of white supremacy includes the hope of an all-white future (even if one cannot return to an 'all-white' past)."[11] Still utilizing notions of past and future, Stone turns to James Baldwin's literary corpus in order to articulate the wisdom found in Baldwin's racial antirealism and his description of white ignorance. In this section, I focus on the term white ignorance and connect it with the metaphor of hell.

According to Stone, Baldwin's description of white ignorance involves four levels. "First," according to Stone, "whites do not know enough about Blacks in proportion to what Blacks know about whites"—which means, "the first level of white ignorance has to do with simply not knowing enough about Black people and their experiences."[12] The second level of white ignorance, what Stone calls a "greater level of ignorance," involves "the form of white parochialism which limits what and how whites can come to understand Blacks."[13] This second level of white ignorance helps make sense of "Baldwin's critique of integration."

> Integration simply moved Blacks into white schools and provided Blacks access to white institutions. The inverse did not happen, which strengthened the [false] idea that whites are at

11. Stone above, 116.

12. Stone above, 118.

13. Stone above, 118.

a higher level than Blacks, and that Blacks were fighting for the opportunity to "move up" to that level. Baldwin accuses whites of not seeing that integration might be an invitation for whites to "move up" to the level of Blacks.[14]

Baldwin is not a critic of integration *per se*, but instead calls into question the assumption that integration means Blacks joining whites rather than whites joining Blacks.

Whereas the first two levels of white ignorance pertain to the ignorance of white people toward Black people, the next two levels concern white self-ignorance. Stone claims that the "tragedy of such ignorance is that it produces a self-ignorance."[15] In Baldwin's words, white people are "still trapped in a history which they do not understand."[16] This level of white ignorance links up with the discussion on the past in the previous section: there is a kind of laziness nurtured by racism in regards to understanding the past. Stone describes this problem as: "White ignorance becomes white not-wanting-to-know-to-tell-the-truth." Stone concludes, "White ignorance involves not only a lack of knowing, but a decision, a decision not-to-know."[17] The apathy and laziness mentioned earlier really do go hand-in-hand because both involve a decision of indifference towards history, the past, and the truth.

And the fourth level of white ignorance concerns confusion over their own decisions. According to Stone, "White ignorance involves the belief that somehow the problems that face Black America have nothing to do with them [white citizens]; they are puzzled that Blacks continue to be angry with the state of things." Stone concludes, "[T]his innocence is . . . part of the ignorance, making white ignorance . . . morally questionable."[18] For Stone, white ignorance is not only an epistemological problem, but also a moral problem.

Putting these levels of white ignorance together result in an overarching ignorance not mentioned by Stone: the fact that racism and white supremacy create societal hells. Because of white ignorance, Black people tend to know they inhabit hell whereas white people remain ignorant of the hell(s) that racism and white supremacy have created. I defend this claim in full by turning to Baldwin's "Down at the Cross."

14. Stone above, 118.
15. Stone above, 118.
16. Baldwin, *The Fire Next Time*, 294.
17. Stone above, 119.
18. Stone above, 119.

Baldwin's "Down at the Cross" and the Metaphor of Hell

In order to defend my claim about the hell(s) created by racism and white supremacy, I shift focus and offer a reading of Baldwin's essay entitled "Down at the Cross"—which is published in *The Fire Next Time* (quoted heavily by Stone as well). My reading utilizes the metaphor of hell for understanding Baldwin's argument in "Down at the Cross." My interpretation of the metaphor of hell for reading Baldwin's "Down at the Cross" includes four points, and for the sake of clarity, I offer headings for each of them: (1) Baldwin and a different type of religious reasoning, (2) from the question of morality to the reality of power, (3) how racism turns Christian virtues into vices, and (4) the relationship between equality, freedom, and power.

Baldwin and a Different Type of Religious Reasoning

Usually when we think of religious reasoning in the context of the US, we tend to think of the ways that American Evangelical Christians and traditionalist Roman Catholics weaponize the name of God in order to justify their own hatred, prejudices, and the systems of oppression that they rely upon. In other words, we tend to think that only conservatives or Republicans employ religious reasoning for defending their political and social views. In "Down at the Cross," however, Baldwin employs religious reasoning in order to help his readers better grasp what's at stake in a racist and white supremacist society.

James Baldwin rightly identifies racism and white supremacy as sin: "For the wages of sin were visible everywhere."[19] Baldwin goes on to describe the personal and societal consequences of the sins of racism and white supremacy. What he describes sounds like hell: a place where love is absent, fear dominates, and madness prevails. What's more is that hatred is called love; fear is justified in the name of safety and security; and madness is considered reasonable.

The police see themselves as guardians, perpetuators, and protectors of the hell that results from the sin of racism and white supremacy: "It was absolutely clear that the police would whip you and take you in as long as they could get away with it."[20] The police are not alone in perpetuating hell: "[E]veryone else—housewives, taxi-drivers, elevator boys, dishwashers, bartenders, lawyers, judges, doctors, and grocers—would never . . . cease

---

19. Baldwin, *The Fire Next Time*, 299.
20. Baldwin, *The Fire Next Time*, 299.

to use you as an outlet for [their] frustrations and hostilities."[21] The sin of racism and white supremacy creates a this-worldly hell for everyone: some people are aware of it while others remain unaware of it. The police, house-wives, taxi-drivers, elevator boys, dishwashers, bartenders, lawyers, judges, doctors, and grocers might be the oppressors, but they too are imprisoned by their own fear, hatred, and ignorance. In a racist and white supremacist society, no one escapes hell.

From the Question of Morality to the Reality of Power

Part of what the metaphor of hell reveals is that no one has moral ground-ing. In Baldwin's words: "white people, who had robbed Black people of their liberty and who profited by this theft every hour that they lived, had no moral ground on which to stand."[22] In hell, everyone gives up their moral code; in hell, morality shifts to a game of power: "They had the judges, the juries, the shotguns, [and] the law—in a word, power."[23] Baldwin clarifies that this version of power ought not be celebrated: "But it was criminal power, to be feared but not respected."[24] Living in hell on earth transforms human relationships from being determined by a sense of morality to being reduced to the reality of domination and power.

How Racism Turns Christian Virtues into Vices

Traditionally, the hope that Christians have in regards to their belief in hell involves Christian salvation. This hope gets expressed through the language of Christian virtue: faith, hope, and charity or love. In the hell created by racism and white supremacy, such language might be preached; what is preached, however, is not practiced.

According to Baldwin, Christians will not be saved from the hell that white Christians created because Christians do not practice their own vir-tues: "I would . . . love to believe that the principles were Faith, Hope, and Charity, but this is clearly not so for most Christians."[25] What do Christians

---

21. Baldwin, *The Fire Next Time*, 299.
22. Baldwin, *The Fire Next Time*, 300.
23. Baldwin, *The Fire Next Time*, 300.
24. Baldwin, *The Fire Next Time*, 300.
25. Baldwin, *The Fire Next Time*, 305.

practice instead of faith, hope, and charity? Baldwin's answer: the principles or vices practiced by Christians are "Blindness, Loneliness, and Terror."[26]

In the "lake of burning brimstone,"[27] American Christianity has sailed far away from the virtue of charity or love: "Christianity has operated with an unmitigated arrogance and cruelty."[28] Traditional Christianity offers the possibility of salvation from societal hell, but American Christianity deepens the hell created by racism and white supremacy. Dante gets it right in the *Inferno*: "those who enter here abandon all hope."[29] Racism and white supremacy lead to hell and hopelessness.[30]

The Relationship between Equality, Freedom, and Power

All of the previous points lead to what might be taken as a surprising conclusion Baldwin draws in "Down at the Cross." Given that we all live in hell, equality and freedom are not what's being asked for by Black Americans. Baldwin argues that Black Americans do not need to be *given* equality and freedom; rather, "The only thing that white people have that black people need, or should want, is power."[31]

Does anyone need to be *given* equality and freedom? Yes, white people do. White people need to be given equality and freedom because white people need to be saved from the hell(s) that they have created. In fact, white people need to be saved from racism and white supremacy: "The price of the liberation of . . . white people is [also] the liberation of the blacks—the total liberation, in the cities, in the towns, before the law, and in the mind."[32] If racism and white supremacy result in a this-worldly hell, then all of us living in this hell require salvation.[33] In other words, there is no white privilege because no one has privilege in hell.

Stone is right to shift from white privilege to *jouissance* and white ignorance, and I take his thinking even further. There is white ignorance in the

26. Baldwin, *The Fire Next Time*, 305.

27. For the phrase "lake of burning brimstone," see Edwards's "Sinners in the Hands of an Angry God."

28. Baldwin, *The Fire Next Time*, 312.

29. See Dante's *Inferno*.

30. For a fictional and literary version of my argument, see Amiri Baraka's novel about racism, entitled *The System of Dante's Hell*.

31. Baldwin, *The Fire Next Time*, 341.

32. Baldwin, *The Fire Next Time*, 342.

33. In Stone's words: "This end of white ignorance will not only free Blacks, it will free white people from their own self-inflicted self-deception" (120).

sense that white people do not see the hell(s) created by racism and white supremacy. The more white people deny that racism and white supremacy create hell for everyone, the more they demonstrate their foolishness and ignorance about the hell(s) created by racism and white supremacy. In hell, no one has equality; in hell, no one has freedom. For there to be equality and freedom for anyone, racism and white supremacy must come to an end. We all need salvation from racism and white supremacy.

This reading of Baldwin's "Down at the Cross" leads to what I explore further in the next section: the problem of white resentment. The problem of white resentment is that it pushes society deeper and further into the hell(s) created by racism and white supremacy. White resentment not only makes its case based upon white ignorance—denying that racism and white supremacy result in hell—but also moves us further and further away from the hope of salvation out of hell.

Kantian Reflections on White Resentment

In chapter 4, I mentioned how much Martin Luther King Jr. worried about white resentment. According to King, anti-racists must remain nonviolent in order for anti-racism not to cause white resentment. To reiterate:

> King worried about white resentment, and he sought through nonviolence to avoid white resentment. While I admire King's conviction on this point, if we have learned anything since 2016—no matter how loving, nonviolent, peaceful, and truthful Black Lives Matter protestors behave—white resentment seems unavoidable. I agree with King that the beloved community turns enemies into "brothers and sisters," but we can no longer assume that the behavior of anti-racists will determine one way or another the resentment of racists and white supremacists.[34]

On the terms Stone develops in chapter 5, King's thinking that anti-racists can determine the behavior of white racists must be considered as "idealist." Is there an alternative?

I explore and suggest a different take and tone on white resentment in this section. Rather than attempt to tie the actions and words of anti-racists with the behavior of white racists, I believe that white resentment makes white people less free. White resentment deepens and furthers the hell(s) created by racism and white supremacy. If white people truly want to be free, white resentment must be dealt with on terms of Enlightenment

34. Goodson above, 74.

philosophy: white resentment involves a version of intellectual immaturity whereas freedom and equality for all requires the achievement of intellectual maturity. In other words, I recommend the application of Immanuel Kant's argument from "What Is Enlightenment?" to the problem of white resentment.

In taking this Kantian approach, I remain close to the language and wisdom of Baldwin's "Down at the Cross." When he introduces the now-famous phrase, "achieving our country," Baldwin writes: "In short, we, the black and the white, deeply need each other . . . if we are really to become a nation—if we are really . . . to achieve our identity, [to achieve] our maturity."[35] Achieving our country will happen only when we "achieve our identity" and achieve intellectual maturity: "If we . . . do not falter in our duty now, we may be able . . . to end the racial nightmare . . . , achieve our country, and change the history of the world."[36] With Baldwin and Kant, I wish to think in terms of achieving our country through achieving intellectual maturity. Intellectual maturity leaves behind the possibility for white resentment.

In "What Is Enlightenment?" Kant opens his essay with a distinction between immaturity and maturity. He says,

> Enlightenment is humanity's emergence from self-incurred immaturity. Immaturity is the inability to use one's own understanding without the guidance of another. This immaturity is self-incurred if its cause is not lack of understanding, but lack of resolution and courage to use it without the guidance of another. The motto of enlightenment is therefore: *Sapere aude!* Have courage to use your own understanding![37]

Racists and white supremacists embrace their immaturity, in the critical sense meant by Kant. In addition to not having a proper understanding, racists and white supremacists lack courage and resolve in terms of telling the truth about the past and the present. Because of their immaturity, we will never "achieve the country" that can be achieved: a country based on actual equality and freedom for all citizens.

In taking this Kantian approach, I also remain close to the language and wisdom of Stone's argument in the previous chapter: how racism nurtures a type of laziness. Stone claims that racism requires laziness about the past: "Indolence, or laziness, is . . . about the impossibility of beginning. Just as anxiety means that one does not know how the future is going to be,

35. Baldwin, *The Fire Next Time*, 342.
36. Baldwin, *The Fire Next Time*, 346–47.
37. Kant, "What Is Enlightenment?," para. 1.

jouissance never does history."[38] According to Kant, one of the vices that accompanies immaturity involves laziness: "Laziness and cowardice are the reasons why such a large proportion of humanity, even when nature has long emancipated them from alien guidance (*naturaliter maiorennes*), nevertheless gladly remain immature for life . . . It is so convenient to be immature!"[39] According to how I understand Stone's use of *jouissance*, Kant's last sentence in this passage resembles Levinasian *jouissance*: "It is so convenient [enjoyable] to be immature!"[40]

In the third paragraph of "What Is Enlightenment?" Kant writes,

> Thus it is difficult for each separate individual to work his way out of the immaturity which has become almost second nature to him. He has even grown fond of it and is really incapable for the time being of using his own understanding, because he was never allowed to make the attempt. Dogmas and formulas, those mechanical instruments for rational use (or rather misuse) of his natural endowments, are the ball and chain of his permanent immaturity. And if anyone did throw them off, he would still be uncertain about jumping over even the narrowest of trenches, for he would be unaccustomed to free movement of this kind. Thus only a few, by cultivating their own minds, have succeeded in freeing themselves from immaturity and in continuing boldly on their way.[41]

Intellectual immaturity becomes second nature to racists and white supremacists. Racism and white supremacy ought to be considered an outdated and problematic dogma that serves as "the ball and chain of [the] permanent immaturity" of racists and white supremacists.[42] Racists and white supremacists claim that they enjoy (*jouissance*) full freedom, but in reality they are imprisoned by their own ideologies and prejudices.

If we follow Baldwin instead of Kant at this point, then we might conclude that what is needed is not Enlightenment but for white people to become more like Black people. However, we do not have to force a dichotomy here: to become mature on the terms of Enlightenment philosophy means becoming Black in the sense described by Stone:

> Baldwin's solution to the agony that white people feel under a racist regime is to become Black. By this Baldwin is not

38. Stone above, 112.
39. Kant, "What Is Enlightenment?," para. 2.
40. Kant, "What Is Enlightenment?," para. 2.
41. Kant, "What Is Enlightenment?," para. 3.
42. Kant, "What Is Enlightenment?," para. 3.

suggesting that one should change their skin color or give up one's way of being. Baldwin is demanding that . . . white people face the realities of their situation and open themselves to . . . the "tragic sense of life." In so doing, we will realize that we are all human, all facing the same problems, and able to live meaningful lives together.[43]

With Baldwin's help, Stone captures what maturity looks like for healing what is broken in a racist and white supremacist society; in other words, Stone describes the substance of our hope out of the hell(s) created by racism and white supremacy. This represents the Enlightenment white people desperately need to experience.

CONCLUSION

I conclude this chapter with autobiographical remarks concerning why I think racism and white supremacy create a hellish society yet still remain hopeful about friendships, personal relationships, and race relations in the US. My junior high days depict both the hellishness and the hope that I have tried to bring out in the analysis and arguments of the current chapter.

I attended a junior high that had close to a 50/50 ratio of Black and white students, perhaps closer to 60/40 with a majority of white students. Somehow, the local KKK developed a strong influence over a small minority of white students in my junior high. The students who had been impacted and influenced by adult members of the KKK in our community decided that the cafeteria should be segregated each day at lunch time. They used intimidation toward white students to discourage them from sitting with Black students, and they used racial slurs toward the Black students to ensure exclusivity and separation. My closest friend at the time (who is also white) and I were two of the biggest bodies in our grade, so we decided that we would stand up to the intimidation and continue to sit with our African American friends at lunchtime. While we were both big bodies, he was actually the tough one whereas I was not (it has taken a lot of psychotherapy sessions for me to be able to admit this about myself). I knew that if their intimidation toward me led to actual aggression and violence, I would not be able to stand up for myself. During one lunch period, this is exactly what happened: outside after eating lunch, I found myself being pushed face first into a metal trash can while being taunted with the words that I was "eating with niggers" and deserved to be punished for it. Despite this incident, I remained determined to continue to sit with my friends.

43. Stone above, 121.

I tell this story neither to ask for sympathy from readers nor to make myself out to be some kind of (white) hero. Rather, I tell the story to say that for a full academic year of my life, a few junior high boys managed to make the experience of lunchtime in the cafeteria an absolute hell for everyone. They served as the guardians of this hell, doing all that they could to make our junior high culture submit to the beliefs of the KKK; they put hateful and unreasonable restrictions on friendships and personal relationships. No one was free—neither Black nor white students—for that year while eating together in the cafeteria. An attempt to sit where one wanted was met with bullying, intimidation, and violence.

I imagine at this point, a reader wonders: Where is the hope? For me, the hope came after school—with football practice in the fall and basketball practice in the spring. What do I mean? (In answering this question, I stick to football because I actually played, whereas I was a benchwarmer on the basketball team!) Almost each—if not all—of the white students that claimed to represent the KKK at my junior high also played football. After they started their racist and segregationist practices in the cafeteria, I remember thinking to myself: How is this going to play out on the football team? While I am not naïve enough to suggest that Black players experienced no racism on the football team (I am certain that they did), I was surprised that the students who promoted the beliefs of the KKK outwardly treated the Black players with the same enthusiasm and respect that they did the white players. For instance, the center on the team was one of the students who promoted the beliefs of the KKK; our quarterback identified as both Black and Latino. Anyone who has played football knows where the hands of the quarterback have to go in relation to the center for hiking the ball each and every play: right up in the butt and crotch area of the center. I was the starting left guard so I served as a firsthand witness of the relationship between the center and quarterback. The center never had any derogatory remarks toward the non-white quarterback having to touch him every single play. Additionally, our running back was an African American (who went on to play running back at the University of Oklahoma, a collegiate team known for its stars at the running back position). The center never blocked with less zeal although he was blocking primarily for two non-white players. Both Black and white players, even the white players who promoted racism and segregation in the cafeteria, butt-slapped and high-fived each other. The segregation in the cafeteria at noon seemed nowhere present on the football practice field at four o'clock.

I am not saying that racism was absent from the football team, but the ideology of the KKK seemed to disappear—at least outwardly—when those white players put on their uniforms. In relation to the hellishness of the cafeteria, the team dynamics of football became my hope for these racist white students. At the time, I thought to myself: if they can bounce their bodies around and into Black players—and even put their own bodies on the line to guard or protect our non-white quarterback and non-white running back—then why can they not have a conversation or share a meal with non-white students? It caused so much dissonance in my fourteen-year-old brain.

In several of his writings, James Baldwin talks about how erotic love between Black and white people ought to lend itself to possibly healing race relations at the societal level. In other words, for Baldwin, what happens in secret in the bathroom between Black and white men or in the bedroom with Black and white heterosexual couples should eventually have some impact at the societal level.[44] Unlike Martin Luther King Jr., Baldwin defends *eros* instead of *agape* as the type of love needed between Black and white people in the US. At fourteen years old, I remember having a similar thought to Baldwin's argument (although I certainly was not thinking about sex in such a hopeful and positive way as Baldwin does): Can the constant interaction of bodies during football practice and the open visibility of bodies in the locker room before and after practice lead to any reconciliation from the pain and suffering being caused by the forced segregation in the cafeteria at lunchtime?

I suppose what I am trying to communicate with this story is that I experienced a type of beloved community being part of the football team, all the while I was daily intimidated and Black students were terrorized by the cultivation of a racist community in the cafeteria. The racism in the cafeteria at lunchtime was a type of hell for all of us, but four hours later the hellishness seemingly disappeared. I realize that this story is only anecdotal, and I recognize that other players might have had a totally different experience on the football team than I describe here. Despite those caveats, I tell the story because it captures a moment in time in my own life where both hellishness and hopefulness were present daily in regards to personal relationships and race relations.

44. For a similar argument about how sex also heals sexism, see de Beauvoir's *The Second Sex*.

Conclusion

Honor, Heroes, Health, Healing, Hope

Philip R. Kuehnert

Where two or three are gathered in my name,
there I am in the midst of them. (Matt 18:20)

HONOR, HEROES, HEALTH, HEALING, HOPE

In early Spring of 2020, a small but determined beloved community located in the Tidewater area of Virginia gathered local and national resources to address the critical issue of racial unrest. The goal was to design, develop, and promote a symposium—building the beloved community in a wounded world. Within a month, that issue was joined by the COVID-19 pandemic crisis. The term *wounded world* seemed to capture the fractured state of affairs from the starkly personal to the global, and the term *beloved community* was a unanimous choice for the ideal that was hoped for by our group. The verb *building* harnessed the energy that galvanizes good people to work for the common good.

To conclude, I humbly return to the five Hs—honor, heroes, health, healing, hope—that provided the structure for the symposium that in the fall of 2020 optimistically presumed to offer a template of sorts for building the beloved community.

Honor

Honor takes on a different meaning, and certainly a different focus, if the community is a beloved community. Despite the limitations of the Zoom platform, the first segment bound participants in a temporary virtual beloved community. Those who so tragically died from COVID-19 as well as those who lost their lives as victims of racial injustice were honored as names were spoken.

Heroes

Within every community or family, occasions will arise that give individuals the opportunity to serve others at the expense of the self. They are honored as heroes. Throughout the Tidewater area and in other parts of the country, banners appeared outside of clinics and hospitals that said "Heroes Work Here." At the Symposium, two women, Tara and Johnette, were identified as heroes because of their work as advocates for social justice issues.

Health

Health is a norm that is defined in wholistic terms. Health is the combination of external forces that maximize well-being and the internal systems of the human body that either allow the person to be fully alive or compromise abundant living. In the symposium, the systemic issues that prevent the equitable delivery of health services were identified. In addition, programs that address those issues were documented and celebrated.

Healing

We know that the body has within it mechanisms to provide healing for the majority of illnesses and injuries. For the increasing number of maladies that threaten our well-being, many of them self or environmentally induced, and not a few because we are living longer, healing has become big business. But its most meaningful form comes as one person, in community, caring for another. Richard Rohr writes, "If we do not transform our pain we will most assuredly transmit it."[1] The symposium presented a healing process that moved from order/health, to disorder, to chaos, to transformation, to new order/health. The beloved community can play an important role in healing and health.

Hope

Finally, the burden and motivation of this book concerns hope. During the symposium, Brad Elliott Stone and Jacob L. Goodson presented the succinct and powerful summary of their ongoing work on hope and the concept of the beloved community. This book captures their presentations and so much more.

AND SO MUCH MORE

Every book to some extent is a reflection of the times during which is it written. This book is no exception. Conceived a week before the 2020 presidential election, I began writing this conclusion on the eve of the transfer of power from one administration to another and finished writing the conclusion as the pandemic in the United States lost its steam (June 12, 2021). The eight months between conception and finishing this book have been among the most dramatic in the past two decades. There was no way to anticipate that, beginning in November, after reaching a plateau midsummer 2020, the pandemic would break loose with what seemed unrelenting terror. Few were aware of the raging malignancy of an alternate reality given cover by the president that would seriously threaten the institutions of the republic. The peaceful transfer of power had become expected, but the events of January 6, 2021, proved the exception to that expectation.

The heartrending reality had to be accepted that racial inequality found its voice in George Floyd's whispered cry, "I can't breathe." Tragically, inequality of all kinds, especially in the delivery of health care services, spelled disproportionate deaths for non-white populations. Pushed out of the headlines was possibly the greatest threat globally, that of the pandemic of crises that threatens life on this planet.

The world is wounded. Grievously. Cries rise! The need for the beloved community to be what it is uniquely qualified to do has never been greater. The time for existing beloved communities to re-examine their effectiveness is now. Beloved communities have within themselves, or easily

---

1. Rohr, "Transforming Pain," para. 2.

accessed resources, what they need for repair and repurpose. The cries of the world, the cries of their countries, and even the cries of children who wonder if there will be an inhabitable world for their grandchildren need to be heard, interpreted, and responded to. As has been made clear in an earlier chapter, the beloved community is not a political organization but has political implications. The failure of organized religion to provide the impetus behind political, judicial, and moral reform is told in the sad stories of temperance laws, pacifist movements, abortion bans, blue laws, and laws designed to keep women "in their place" and white supremacists in power. The challenge of avoiding political polarization continues.

However, the track record of beloved communities as being the incubators of individuals who have been torch bearers in almost every field of endeavors that have made the world a better place is remarkable. While the focus of the beloved community is primarily on building and maintaining itself, the beloved community that forgets its role in the world abandons its commitment to make a difference in the world. Historically, that commission has been tragically misdirected in imperialist ambition, crusades, wars, colonization, genocide, and what seems to be endemic caste systems. Those horrific mistakes are no excuse for the beloved communities of all three Abrahamic traditions to fail to use the philosophical and theological resources now available to build, renovate, and repair beloved communities in order to respond to the cries of the wounded world. The beloved community is called to follow those cries, and the cries are not new.

It is the kind of thinking, not only by Goodson and Stone but by many of their peers who have taken on themselves a certain type of prophetic reasoning, that provides the critical voice to revitalize the arguments in new and exciting ways about what is good, just, and true. It is not by accident that they and their intellectual mentors speak of virtues that present an ideal of what the beloved community should be and can become. The move to prophetic pragmatism gathers thinkers like them: from James Baldwin, Martin Luther King Jr., and Emmanuel Levinas, to Joy James, Peter Ochs, and Cornel West. These names represent thinkers and writers who commit themselves to building beloved community and the hard lifting that needs to be accomplished so that the cries of the world can be heard. More than that, as I have argued, the beloved community is ideally the place where the wounded are welcomed with whatever "waste howling wilderness" envelops them.[2] Within the community, they find refuge and manna.

Within the beloved community, there will always be those with wounds, horrific, bleeding literally or spiritually/psychically—those who

---

2. See Washington, *Conversations*, 169.

are put at risk by life-threatening infections and always those who carry scars, invisible to the uncaring eye, but visible to those who listen with finely tuned ears. Realistically, our wounded world is also a wounding world, and the beloved community is challenged to be a healing presence in that world.

WOUNDS, SCABS, AND SCARS

Emergency rooms are famous for gore, for heroic efforts, and for the saddest moments in people's lives. Because we live in a wounded/wounding world, where safety is a seldom realized ideal, the beloved community by necessity is required to provide a special kind of emergency service and more. So much more.

"What doesn't kill you will make you stronger." Reality says that finally "something" will kill you, no matter how many times escaping death meant becoming a stronger person. While death has always been a part of life, there have been major efforts to bring death back into the public square. After several decades of denying death, the mid-twentieth century was forced to respond because of events that could not be ignored. These events evoked responses that countered the denial of death. First among these was war: WWII, Korea, Vietnam, Afghanistan. Second were the domestic events: statistics of cardiovascular disease caused by tobacco, 9/11, the escalating number of deaths due to gun violence, and state-sanctioned death—currently under challenge by the Black Lives Matter movement. Hospice and the rise of palliative care as a medical specialty became a necessary response to the inevitability and visibility of death.

The beloved community draws from elaborate and well-established traditions and rituals that mark the mystery and sanctity of death. Professionals and volunteers are expected to provide for the "expired remains" as well as the survivors who grieve. Death is normalized. Death is planned for through life insurance, wills, trusts, estate planning, and expensive buy-ins to multi-level care facilities where relatively healthy older folks go to enjoy the last stages of life with the assurance that they will be cared for with dignity until death. The dead are remembered and/or celebrated with wakes and funerals and celebrations of life, obituaries, tombstones, memorials, endowed chairs, named buildings, and named foundations.

It is the connection between the beloved community and the important role that it plays in the last stage of life that is often lost. It is not lost for those who live their lives within the context of the beloved community, but it is lost for those whose primary communities are not beloved communities. The specific term, the beloved community—as described by Josiah Royce and adopted by Martin Luther King Jr.—has been used as an ideal by the planning committee of the James River Chapter of the Virginia Interfaith Center for Public Policy. In this book, beloved community has been used as a potential response to political divisiveness in the US.

Somewhat new is the emphasis on the role that the beloved community plays in the healing process from wounds to scabs and finally scars. Again, several events have refocused attention on the role the beloved community plays in the no-longer-simple, straight-line healing sequence of wound to scab to scar. While soft tissue, muscle, and skin may predictably move from wound to scab to scar, that progression is often fitful at best and delayed or halted at worst. It is in this transition that a variety of infections pose a real or even fatal threat. Among those events is the attention forced upon our society and its support systems to face the reality of what trauma science has revealed. The reality of post-traumatic stress disorder crippling survivors is no longer debated. The life-altering effects of traumatic brain injury has been recognized for decades. Recently, CTE (Chronic Traumatic Encephalopathy), the tragic consequence of repeated concussions suffered by professional boxers, hockey players, and football players, has received outsized media attention because of the hundreds of millions of dollars being paid to settle lawsuits. Homeless, nomads, chronically mentally ill and the generational effects of four-hundred years of systemic racism focused on people of color, selected minorities, and indigenous peoples together witness to a world that inflicts lasting wounds.

Participating in the local Natural History Museum's volunteer day, we met a retired county agent who works at the museum each Wednesday morning. In conversation with him, after we completed our work, he commented on how "community" seems to come together on its own. He referred to a Quaker group that had met via Zoom during the pandemic as well as a group of farmers from Missouri that he meets with on Monday evenings for centering prayer. Habitat for Humanity is an excellent example of how a faith-based organization has provided thousands of local beloved communities the opportunity to put God's love into action in their own communities while expanding community beyond the often inward-focused local beloved community.

As noted earlier, the word "building" is the nitroglycerin in this book. From the opening salvo, the intent has been to challenge the reader to think deeply about the unique characteristics of our wounded world and to consider new ways of thinking about the necessary components of a beloved community.

Although this book was not intended to be in any way a treatise on theodicy, it is difficult at this point to think of the arguments of this book as being anything but a way to defend and acknowledge a God who hears and who, in the anointed beloved community, provides surrogate ears. If the church, or the primitive desire for the human to live in community, is part of the divine plan, the building of the beloved community, or the gathering of community in whatever form, becomes a necessity for survival. In these tortured and always challenging arguments, the resulting cry is anticipated by the prophet who screams,

> Oh, that you would rend the heavens and come down,
>   that the mountains would tremble before you!
> Since ancient times no one has heard,
>   no ear has perceived,
> no eye has seen any God besides you,
>   who acts on behalf of those who wait for him.
> You come to the help of those who gladly do right,
>   who remember your ways. (Isa 64:1, 4–5)

So what about the one holy Christian and apostolic church? What about the categories of the church triumphant and the church militant, or the church visible and invisible? What about the various polities that govern the various expressions of the Christian church? It would seem to be an unfortunate omission to refuse to address the relation of the holy Christian church to the beloved community as described in this book. Church polities range from the authoritarian top-down episcopal model to the bottom-up congregational model to models that attempt to follow what suggestions there are in the New Testament about congregational structure. It is not a stretch to say that all work and that all have proven at times to be disastrous. The particular structure seems less important than the integrity of the people who are in charge of the various functions of the congregation.

Since before the Reformation, there was constant unrest with the church under the unified umbrella of the Church at Rome. The Reformation of the fifteenth and sixteenth centuries gave rise to several polities that have shown remarkable endurance. In contemporary Christendom, traditional polities—such as the presbytery, congregational, and episcopal models—are challenged by a variety of hybrid models that are found in non-denominational churches, so-called megachurches, and charismatic or Pentecostal denominations. Under traditional banners like Baptist, Lutheran, and Methodist are literally hundreds of denominations, in which worshiping communities as few as two and as many as several thousands have bound themselves together for the many purposes, practical, theological, and ethnic. From this book's perspective, all of these polities are capable of hosting beloved communities. In fact, if there is such a thing as a unifying self-understanding of all of these organized expressions of Christianity, it would be that all would suppose themselves to be beloved communities.

THE BELOVED COMMUNITY

The beloved communities that have always provided succor, respite, and healing continue to meet challenges for which they are uniquely qualified. The ideal beloved community is under pressure to adapt to new ways of providing those things that it only can provide in a changing and ever newly wounded world. The beloved community by its very nature continues as an ongoing process of building and renovation. With that in mind, it is difficult to imagine a functioning beloved community in a wounded and wounding world without, minimally, the following:

- The self-understanding that the beloved community is at the same time wilderness and refuge.

- Emergency and rehabilitation services (see "Wounds, Scabs, and Scars" above).

- A polity—an organizational structure, a decision-making process, a transparent chain of authority, and a process—that details who is in and who is out.

- A place where *words of Scripture* are given a place of honor, where the texts are studied and argued over, and where sermons are preached and lessons are taught.

- A place where *words of prayer* provide the ongoing chronicling of the community's life, where the dynamic of prayer chains, prayer meetings, and prayer partners may add the dimension of God's ears to the community, and where personal disciplines of prayer are encouraged.

- A place where *music and song* capture in another dimension the words of Scripture and prayer.

- A place where the numinous meets reality in *sacraments of water, bread, and wine.*

- A place and time where the above happens, called *worship/meeting*, where people in real time gather and obediently listen, speak, and sing; where in story, liturgy, and tradition the wounded world is welcomed and the promulgation of pious platitudes is prohibited; where the opening and closing stanzas are always about hope; where the tragic sense of life and life in all its abundance live together in harmony.

- Personnel as beloved communities grow. Job descriptions and qualifications for specific roles are established, and candidates are called, appointed, contracted, or hired. Precedent for this extends to the qualifications listed in the New Testament, beginning with the choosing of seven people from among the number, people of good reputation, full of the Spirit and of wisdom to assist the apostles (Acts 6:1–7). In addition, the pastoral epistles list extended qualifications for those chosen to be bishops and elders in the New Testament church. Even moderate-sized worshiping communities will often have additional church staff in addition to the pastor.

- Governance (different from polity). Throughout my fifty years of being involved in Lutheran worshiping communities, I experienced three different forms of governance in which specific ministries were organized and legal and financial guidelines were prescribed. The primary difference in the three structures was how volunteer and paid personnel were supervised. As one form of governance followed the next, the argument was always that the mission of the congregation would be enhanced by the new. In retrospect, whether one form of structure facilitated the beloved community more than others is now for me an open question.

- Theology. If the above is not messy enough, add to this the confusion over how God is involved and directs. Additionally, how and to what extent the Bible and/or tradition determines ministry adds to the messiness. Whether explicit or implicit, every worshiping community has a purpose. In more sophisticated worshiping communities, there will be slogans that in a couple of words capture its identity, a catchy mission statement that identifies an organizing principal and then a variety of goals and objectives and values and priorities, etc., which are used as recruitment tools and markers for what the community does.

BUILDING, RENOVATING, MAINTAINING

It is the building that challenges. Building requires vision. Vision requires thinking. Thinking involves the messiness of philosophy and theology. This book, above all else, is a book about thinking. Thinking involves words. From chapters 1 of Genesis and John's Gospel, the word and the Word provide the creative forces for beginnings. Words invite thinking, interpretation, and argument.

However, it is the maintaining and renovating of the beloved community that demands equal if not more attention. As anyone who has gone through renovation or remodeling knows, messiness cannot be avoided.

I have written my chapters and this conclusion in my study that sits above the garage overlooking a small cul-de-sac that encircles a small park. Directly across, in the setting sun, I look on the building site of five conjoined patio homes. Since mid-December, when we were informed that those lots had been chosen for the patio homes, I have witnessed the building process that began the week before Christmas with staking out the footprint. On January 4, equipment moved in. Activity did not stop until trenches were dug and footers were poured. It was ugly, muddy, and messy. Now, six months later I look out and see the framed and roofed shell of five patio homes. The shell conceals some heating and air conditioning work and some roughed-in electrical work, but what I see has not changed for three months. Vans come and go fitfully. Two months ago, a neighbor in the know confided in me that there had been a glitch in the construction. For two weeks, workers came and went. The sound of saws and hammers reached my aerie. Debris was carried out and new material carried in. Little has been done in the past three weeks. Supply chain issues and shortages of workers in the trades have slowed building. Ironically, the sun at this moment is shining through a framed stained glass that hangs in the window overlooking the building site. The stained glass is a depiction of the iconic image of Jesus with a lantern knocking on a door. I wonder . . .

As Christians, we struggle personally with Jesus—his presence if not his divinity. We even struggle with the question of transcendence. Yet, as surely as I know that deep thinking, accumulated in architecture, engineering, and the building trades will by the end of the summer, or maybe the fall, combine to produce safe habitable space for five occupants, so am I convinced that deep thinking, informed by history and the accumulation of wisdom, will make building the beloved community a reality for a time. A beloved community may survive a couple of weeks, months, or by some ingenuity, grace, and grit, decades or even centuries. But not forever.

Building the beloved community is an ongoing and always messy endeavor. No one or no group, as far as I know, has gotten it right. But through the centuries, despite inherent messiness, some beloved communities have survived—most notably the local worshiping communities who have periodically exemplified the best of the beloved community.

The three of us are wounded refugees who have from time to time basked in the glow of the best of what a beloved community can offer. We also know the pain when the beloved community becomes a toxic community. We are aware of the "waste howling wilderness," for we have been there with family and worshiping community.[3] Where is refuge to be found? Safety, justice, and equality are ideals that will never be totally realized. While we believe the beloved community provides a place of refuge, we know that even the Beloved Community struggles with safety, justice, and equality. We echo Simon Peter's poignant, "Lord, to whom shall we go . . . ?" (John 5:68).

Depending on who you are, reading this book promised contrasting experiences. Those conversant with current American philosophy and/or who have some competence in theology and pastoral care will have found this book challenging and inspiring. For those whose interests and orientation are primarily philosophical, Stone's and Goodson's chapters should provide material for vibrant arguments. For those who come primarily from a Christian point of view grounded in a local worshiping congregation, the opening salvo, chapters 3 and 6, and this conclusion should provide the motivation to do a vigorous analysis of the beloved community you might call your own. For the intensely focused, the book—whether in philosophy, theology, or the sociology of religion—will have been frustrating. The trained theologian and the lay theologian will be most frustrated.[4]

Investment in, participation within, and deep thinking and vigorous debate about the Beloved Community brings the promise that God will not abandon those who seek to be in God's presence.

3. See Washington, *Conversations*, 169.

4. For those, I recommend reading Paul R. Hinlicky's two volumes which address the topic of the Beloved Community, *Beloved Community: Critical Dogmatics after Christendom*, and *Luther and the Beloved Community*.

Bibliography

Appiah, Anthony Kwame. *The Ethics of Identity*. Princeton: Princeton University Press, 2007.

Baldwin, James. *The Evidence of Things Not Seen*. Ann. ed. New York: Picador, 1995.

———. *James Baldwin: Collected Essays*. Edited by Toni Morrison. Washington, DC: Library of America, 1998.

Baraka, Amiri. *The System of Dante's Hell*. New York: Akashic, 2016.

Bonhoeffer, Dietrich. *Life Together: The Classic Exploration of Christian Community*. New York: Harper One, 1954.

Bowler, Kate. *Everything Happens for a Reason: And Other Lies I've Loved*. New York: Random House, 2018.

Bussie, Jacqueline A. *Outlaw Christian Finding Authentic Faith by Breaking the Rules*. Rumson: Nelson, 2016.

Caruth, Cathy. *Unclaimed Experience: Trauma, Narrative, and History*. Baltimore: John Hopkins University Press, 1996.

Chugh, Amy. *The Person You Mean to Be: How Good People Fight Bias*. New York: HarperCollins, 2018.

Collier, Charlie, et al. "Introduction." In *Unsettling Arguments*, edited by Charles R. Pinches, Kelly S. Johnson, and Charles M. Collier, ix–xvii. Eugene, OR: Cascade, 2010.

Dante Alighieri. *The Divine Comedy, Vol. 1: Inferno*. New York: Penguin, 1992.

de Beauvoir, Simone. *The Second Sex*. Translated by Constance Borde and Sheila Malovany-Chevallier. New York: Vintage, 2011.

Drabinski, John. "James Baldwin: Democracy between Nihilism and Hope." In *African American Political Thought: A Collected* History, edited by Melvin Rogers and Jack Turner, 481–96. Chicago: University of Chicago Press, 2021.

Edwards, Jonathan. "Sinners in the Hands of an Angry God." *Voices of Democracy*, July 15, 2006. http://voicesofdemocracy.umd.edu/edwards-sinners-in-the-hands-speech-text/.

Ford, David F. *Christian Wisdom Desiring God and Learning in Love*. Cambridge: Cambridge University Press, 2007.

Forster, Walter O. *Zion on the Mississippi: The Settlement of the Saxon Lutherans in Missouri, 1839–1941*. St. Louis: Concordia, 1953.

Goodson, Jacob L., and Brad Elliott Stone. *Introducing Prophetic Pragmatism: A Dialogue on Hope, the Philosophy of Race, and the Spiritual Blues*. Lanham: Lexington, 2019.

Goodson, Jacob L. *The Dark Years?: Philosophy, Politics, and the Problem of Predictions*. Eugene, OR: Cascade, 2020.

——. "Peter Ochs and the Purpose of Philosophy." In *Signs of Salvation*, edited by Mark James and Randi Rashkover, 95–104. Eugene, OR: Cascade, 2021.

——. *The Philosopher's Playground: Understanding Scriptural Reasoning through Modern Philosophy*. Eugene, OR: Cascade, 2021.

——. "The Psalms of Vengeance: Dietrich Bonhoeffer's Theological Interpretation of the Psalms." *Journal of Scriptural Reasoning* 12, no. 1 (November 2013). https://jsr.shanti. virginia.edu/back-issues/vol-12-no-1-november-2013-music-the-psalms-and-scriptural-reasoning/the-psalms-of-vengeance-dietrich-bonhoeffers-theological-interpretation-of-the-psalms/.

——. *Strength of Mind: Courage, Hope, Freedom, Knowledge*. Eugene, OR: Cascade, 2018.

Haidt, Jonathan. *The Righteous Mind: Why Good People Are Divided by Politics and Religion*. New York: Pantheon, 2021.

Hinlicky, Paul R. *Beloved Community Critical Dogmatics after Christendom*. Grand Rapids: Eerdmans, 2015.

——. *Luther and the Beloved Community: A Path for Christian Theology after Christendom*. Grand Rapids: Eerdmans, 2012.

Hook, Sidney. "Pragmatism and the Tragic Sense of Life." *Proceedings and Addresses of the American Philosophical Association* 33 (1959–1960) 5–26.

James, Joy. *Seeking the Beloved Community: A Feminist Race Reader*. Albany: SUNY, 2014.

James, William. "The Moral Philosopher and the Moral Life." In *Will to Believe and Other Popular Essays*, 184–215. New York: Dover, 1959.

——. "On a Certain Blindness in Human Beings." In *Talks to Teachers on Psychology and to Students on Some of Life's Ideals*, 113–29. New York: Dover, 2001.

——. *Pragmatism*. New York: Dover, 1995.

——. *The Varieties of Religious Experience: A Study in Human Nature*. New York: New American Library, 1958.

Jones, Serene. *Trauma and Grace: Theology in a Ruptured World*. 2nd ed. Louisville: Westminster John Know Press, 2019.

Kant, Immanuel. "What Is Enlightenment?" *Columbia University*. http://www.columbia. edu/acis/ets/CCREAD/etscc/kant.html.

King, Martin Luther. "Birth of a New Nation." In *The Papers of Martin Luther King Jr., Vol. IV: Symbol of the Movement, January 1957–December 1958*, edited by Clayborne Carson et al., 155–67. Stanford: University of California Press, 2000.

——. "The Role of the Church in Facing the Nation's Chief Moral Dilemma." In *The Papers of Martin Luther King Jr., Vol. IV: Symbol of the Movement, January 1957–December 1958*, edited by Clayborne Carson et al., 184–91. Stanford: University of California Press, 2000.

van der Kolk, Bessel. *The Body Keeps the Score: Brain, Mind, and Body in the Healing of Trauma*. New York: Penguin, 2014.

Kuklick, Bruce. *Josiah Royce: An Intellectual Biography*. New York: Bobbs-Merrill Company, 1972.

Lakoff, George. *The ALL NEW Don't Think of an Elephant!: Know Your Values and Frame the Debate*. White Water Junction: Chelsea Green, 2014.

Levinas, Emmanuel. *Ethics and Infinity: Conversations with Philippe Nemo*. Translated by Richard A. Cohen. Pittsburgh: Duquesne University Press, 1985.

―――. *Otherwise than Being, or Beyond Essence*. Translated by Alphonso Lingis. Pittsburgh: Duquesne University Press, 1998.

―――. "Philosophy and the Idea of the Infinite." In *Collected Philosophical Papers*, translated by Alphonso Lingis, 47–60. Pittsburgh: Duquesne University Press, 1987.

―――. *Totality and Infinity: An Essay on Exteriority*. Translated by Alphonso Lingis. Pittsburgh: Duquesne University Press, 1969.

Lutheran Book of Worship. Minneapolis: Augsburg Fortress, 1978.

Lutheran Church Missouri Synod. *Lutheran Service Book*. St. Louis: Concordia, 2005.

Marsh, Charles. *The Beloved Community: How Faith Shapes Social Justice from the Civil Rights Movement to Today*. New York: Basic, 2006.

Niedner, Frederick. "Lament and Sustenance in the COVID-19 Wilderness." Presentation at Lutheran School of Theology, Chicago, IL, online session, June 2020.

Ochs, Peter. *Peirce, Pragmatism, and the Logic of Scripture*. Cambridge: Cambridge University Press, 2005.

Parker, Kelly. "Josiah Royce." In *The Stanford Encyclopedia of Philosophy*, edited by Edward N. Zalta. Stanford: Metaphysics Research Lab, 2020.

Peirce, Charles Sanders. "Evolutionary Love." In *The Essential Peirce, Vol. 1: Selected Philosophical Writings, 1867–1893*, edited by Nathan Houser and Christian Kloesel, 352–72. Bloomington: Indiana University Press, 1992.

―――. "A Guess at the Riddle." In *Collected Papers of Charles S. Peirce, Vol. 1*, edited by Charles Hartshorne, 166–203. Cambridge: Belknap, 1932.

Philström, Sami. "The Cries of the Wounded in *Pragmatism*: The Problem of Evil and James's Pragmatic Method as an Ethical Grounding of Metaphysics." In *William James, Moral Philosophy, and the Ethical Life*, edited by Jacob L. Goodson, 297–316. Lanham: Lexington, 2018.

Putnam, Hilary. *The Collapse of the Fact/Value Dichotomy*. Cambridge: Harvard University Press, 2004.

Rohr, Richard. "Transforming Pain: A Daily Meditation." *Center for Action and Contemplation*, October 17, 2018. https://cac.org/transforming-pain-2018-10-17/.

Rorty, Richard. *Consequences of Pragmatism*. Minneapolis: University of Minnesota Press, 1982.

―――. *Contingency, Irony, and Solidarity*. Cambridge: Cambridge University Press, 1989.

―――. *Objectivity, Relativism, and Truth: Philosophical Papers, Vol. 1*. Cambridge: Cambridge University Press, 1991.

―――. *Philosophy and the Mirror of Nature*. Princeton: Princeton University Press, 1979.

―――. *Philosophy and Social Hope*. New York: Penguin, 1998.

―――. "The Prophet and the Professor: A Review of Cornel West's 'American Evasion of Philosophy.'" *Transition* 52 (1991) 70–78.

Royce, Josiah. *The Philosophy of Josiah Royce*. Edited by John Roth. New York: Crowell, 1971.

―――. *The Problem of Christianity*. Washington, DC: Catholic University of America Press. 2001.

―――. *The Religious Aspect of Philosophy: A Critique of the Bases of Conduct and of Faith*. New York: Houghton Mifflin, 1885.

―――. *Sources of Religious Insight*. New York: Octagon, 1977.

———. *The Spirit of Modern Philosophy: An Essay in the Form of Lectures*. New York: Dover, 2015.

Seigfried, Charlene Haddock. *Pragmatism and Feminism: Reweaving the Social Fabric*. Chicago: University of Chicago Press, 1996.

Shanks, Andrew. *Hegel vs. "Inter-faith Dialogue": A General Theory of True Xenophilia*. Cambridge: Cambridge University Press, 2015.

Stone, Brad Elliott. "Making Religious Practices Intelligible: A Prophetic Pragmatic Interpretation of Radical Orthodoxy." *Contemporary Pragmatism* 1, no. 2 (December 2004) 137–53.

———. "Making Religious Practices Intelligible in the Public Sphere: A Pragmatist Evaluation of Scriptural Reasoning." *Journal of Scriptural Reasoning* 10, no. 2 (December 2011). https://jsr.shanti.virginia.edu/back-issues/volume-10-no-2-december-2011-public-debate-and-scriptural-reasoning/making-religious-practices-intelligible-in-the-public-sphere.

Sullivan, Shannon. *Good White People: The Problem with Middle-Class White Anti-Racism*. Albany: SUNY, 2014.

Trotter, Griffin. *On Royce*. Belmont: Wadsworth, 2001.

Unamuno, Miguel de. *Tragic Sense of Life*. Translated by J.E. Crawford Flitch. New York: Dover, 1954.

Ward, Roger. "The Cries of the Wounded: Transformative Moral Interpretation in James, Peirce, and Royce" In *William James, Moral Philosophy, and the Ethical Life*, edited by Jacob L. Goodson, 89–96. Lanham: Lexington, 2018.

Washington, James Melvin. *Conversations with God Two Centuries of Prayers by African Americans*. New York: HarperCollins, 1994.

West, Cornel. *The American Evasion of Philosophy*. Madison: University of Wisconsin Press, 1989.

———. *The Cornel West Reader*. New York: Civitas, 1999.

———. *Democracy Matters: Winning the Fight Against Imperialism*. New York: Penguin, 2005.

———. *The Ethical Dimensions of Marxist Thought*. New York: Monthly Review, 1991.

———. *Keeping Faith: Philosophy and Race in America*. New York: Routledge, 1993.

———. "Philosophy and the Afro-American Experience." *Philosophical Forum* 9 (1977–1978) 117–48.

———. *Prophesy Deliverance!: An Afro-American Revolutionary Christianity*. Philadelphia: Westminster John Knox Press, 1982.

———. "Review of *Philosophy and the Mirror of Nature* by Richard Rorty." *Union Seminary Quarterly Review* 37, no. 1–2 (1981–1982) 179–85.

———. *Sketches from My Culture*. Crystal Clear Studio, 2001, compact CD.

———. *Street Knowledge*. Roc Diamond Records, 2005, compact CD.

West, Cornel, and Henry Louis Gates. *The Future of the Race*. New York: Knopf, 1996.

West, Cornel, and John Rajchman, eds. *Post-Analytic Philosophy*. New York: Columbia University Press, 1985.

Winnicott, D.W. *Playing and Reality*. New York: Routledge, 1971.

Young, William W., III. *Listening, Religion, and Democracy in Contemporary Boston*. Lanham: Lexington, 2018.

Name Index

Subject Index

Made in the USA
Middletown, DE
06 July 2023